Decolonizing Rhetoric and Composition Studies

Iris D. Ruiz • Raúl Sánchez
Editors

Decolonizing Rhetoric and Composition Studies

New Latinx Keywords for Theory and Pedagogy

Editors
Iris D. Ruiz
University of California - Merced
Merced, California, USA

Raúl Sánchez
University of Florida
Gainesville, Florida, USA

ISBN 978-1-137-52723-3   ISBN 978-1-137-52724-0   (eBook)
DOI 10.1057/978-1-137-52724-0

Library of Congress Control Number: 2016947980

Cover illustration: © RTimages/Alamy Stock Photo

Printed on acid-free paper

This Palgrave Macmillan imprint is published by Springer Nature
The registered company is Nature America Inc. New York

FOREWORD

Keywords. The editors will tell us that this is what this book is about—keywords in consideration of the decolonial imaginary. So let me do my part, by way of whetting your appetites for the chapters that follow by looking at three words: "postcolonial," "decolonial," and the reason for my referring to "the imaginary."

We tend to know of postcolonialism within rhetoric, thanks in part to the work of Andrea Lunsford, who is cited in the pages that follow. And, of course, we know those from other disciplines whose work refers specifically to the postcolonial. At least a couple of the decolonial's major figures have found their way into our conversations, mainly Enrique Dussel and Walter Mignolo. But, really, "the decolonial" is a term new to us in Rhetoric and in Composition Studies. So how are the post- and the de- different? In some sense, they aren't very much. The postcolonial arises from political decisions following World War II, when much of South Asia and much of Africa were released from classical colonial control. In addition, most of what we seem attracted to, because of its explicit tie to rhetoric and the English language, comes from South Asia (an oversimplification, I know, but it'll serve).

Although neither Edward Said nor Frantz Fanon is South Asian, they get at a basic element of the postcolonialism in Said's rendering of Fanon's use of a kind of secular Manichaeism. That rendering of Manichaeism established something of a binary between the colonizer and the colonized, in which the colonizer was clearly the *One* and the colonized the *Other*. Any self-perceived strengths of the One were reflected as its opposite in the Other, as in "normal" versus "colored," for example. This is perhaps best known through the Subaltern Studies Group—subalterns as in those whom Gayatri Spivak thought could not have a voice of their own in the context of colonialism—those who would always instead be spoken for.

In some sense, the decolonial is not very much different, although geography and history and culture(s) mark major differences. The decolonial is probably best marked by *el Grupo Modernidad/Decolonialidad*, which includes Walter Mignolo and Anibal Quijano, both of whom are also mentioned in the chapters that follow. But where the colonized were Othered in postcolonial South Asia and Africa, the indigenous of this hemisphere were to be eliminated, not only Othered but removed, either physically or culturally in a long and relatively successful campaign of genocide of one kind or other, giving rise to efforts about which we will read to rediscover buried histories and rhetorics, and giving rise to the need for alliances with Indigenous Studies—again matters to be discussed in what follows. Although the term *decolonial* is more recent than *postcolonial*, the decolonial's history goes much farther back.

That history complicates the very idea of a true "delinking," *delinking* being another keyword you will be reading about quite a bit here. It is in a very real sense difficult to imagine a *de-* any more than a true *post-*. But it becomes important to grapple with the complications, to begin to form some notion of decolonization in our collective imaginary (by which I don't really wish to invoke Lacan's "imaginary," only the fact that we have to imagine the possibility). We live in a global economic and even, to a great extent, cultural world system, all of us tied to all of us, yet subject to global hegemony, not so much in terms of ruling nation-states but in terms of cultures and economies and the seeming control of information in the information age.

Consider, for example, the arguments that we will read asserting the indignity of English-Only legislation. It becomes an assertion of a right to choose which colonizer we will honor: Will we be confined to English? Or will we assert the language of this hemisphere's first European colonizers? If Spanish, will the world of commerce insist on one dialect over another, attempts at "brown-washing" (as opposed to whitewashing) the various indigenous tongues that have inflected our dialects? Complicated stuff.

Or, consider the case of Puerto Rico, again in the news as I write this, as the Island stands at the brink of bankruptcy despite being owned by the

United States. The United Nations Special Committee on Decolonization, for instance, continues to call on the United States to get on with letting Puerto Rico go. But the rhetoric says that Puerto Ricans of the Island (because there are more of us who continue to claim Puerto Rico within the continental US than on the Island) have consistently voted for continued colonial status or, more recently, statehood. For all that, true independence means becoming a neocolonial subject of the World Bank whose members also must be part of the International Monetary Fund, headquartered in Washington, DC. And statehood means the end of US federal subsidies to people who can't find work because there are no jobs. As a state, Puerto Rico would have to take on subsidizing its people, an Island going bankrupt despite being a part of the United States.

But what's most interesting is the assertion that the people of Puerto Rico, we're told, voted for statehood in a November 2012 referendum. Here's the thing, though. Seventy-eight percent of the people voted on a two-part referendum. Part One asked if the people wished to maintain their current colonial status; 54 % said no. Part Two asked, then, if not the status quo, then statehood or independence or *Sovereign Free Associated State*. That particular designation, Sovereign Free Associated State, would be a quasicolony. Unlike their current status, Puerto Ricans would have their own citizenship but with unfettered access to the United States (no visa requirements); the government of Puerto Rico would be free to engage in international trade (which is currently forbidden), but it would still be able to enjoy US military protection and the protection of continued US federal subsidies. This is the status of America's colonies in the Pacific—the Marshall Islands. Thing is, the US Constitution disallows this option for Puerto Rico, so the vote was a set-up, which gave rise to 26 % of that 78 % who voted on Part One refusing to vote on Part Two because the only bona-fide options were, then, statehood or the status quo. Because non-votes can't be counted as votes, the majority of votes went for statehood, but not by the majority of those voting.

But my point in all of this is that all of the options amounted to variations on colonization. The indigenous, Latinxs, and Latin Americans of this hemisphere really do not have a *de*colonial option—in that we are subject to English or to Spanish, subject to racism, subject to world trade in what is essentially an oligopoly, and the like. Yet we cannot simply throw up our hands. And we can't simply react willy-nilly to every slight or injustice, as they are so many and in some sense all of a piece. We have to think our ways through this problem of status—economic, cultural, semiotic (in Mignolo's sense, as we'll read), think our ways through with all of the people of our disciplines, our world, who see the injustices and would want them righted.

Colonialism remains, despite the *post-* and the *de-*. It's a knotty problem. In the pages that follow attempts are made to lay out the problems so that we might begin to untie the knots.

Victor Villanueva
Pullman, WA
14 August 2015

Contents

LIST OF FIGURES

INTRODUCTION: DELINKING

This book brings together twenty-first century Latinx scholars in the field of Rhetoric and Composition to both claim and reclaim important conceptual terms that have been misused or appropriated by institutional, hegemonic forces working against the interests of minority students. In educational and political forums, for example, rhetorics of identity and civil rights have been used to justify ideas and policies that reaffirm the myth of a normative US culture that is white, Eurocentric, and monolinguistically English. These attempts amount to a de facto project of epistemic neocolonization, if we understand "colonization" to include not only the taking of land but also the taking of culture and the defining of knowledge (of which language is a crucial part).

Here are two examples directly related to education:

- In 2007, writing for the plurality in *Parents Involved in Community Schools v. Seattle School District No. 1*, U.S. Supreme Court Chief Justice John Roberts explains, in part, the court's decision to strike down as unconstitutional the school district's racial tiebreaker system for distributing students across schools: "the way to stop discrimination on the basis of race is to stop discriminating on the basis of race."
- In 2010, Arizona House Bill 2281, which bans from the K–12 curriculum courses in Mexican American Studies and Ethnic Studies, declares that students should be "taught to treat and value each other as individuals and not be taught to resent or hate other races or classes of people."

In the first case, Roberts adopted the rhetoric of civil rights—specifically, the ideal of color-blindness—to justify a legal interpretation that, in effect, perpetuates systemic discrimination based precisely on color. Similarly, the language of House Bill 2281 denounces the racism that is the very target of the curriculum it seeks to ban. We find this rhetoric in other public arenas, as well. It directly and indirectly attacks the modest political, economic, and educational progress made by Latinxs and other people of color since the 1960s. It is often persuasive and powerful, leading to action that does lasting harm and inflicts real pain.

From an academic perspective—from the perspective of theory, research, and pedagogy into writing and rhetoric—what is required, and what we propose in this book, is to invoke and examine language that will bring the field of Composition and Rhetoric closer to issues that are relevant to Latinxs' experiences. Specifically, we have two main goals: (1) to argue for an *epistemic delinking* from the falsely universalized notions of rhetoric that have accompanied Western Modernity's spread across this hemisphere, and (2) to offer examples of this delinking in action through detailed work on specific terms. Contributors to this volume draw on their training in rhetorics, and, often, on their own experiences as people of color, in order to reset the scholarly agenda for the future. We reclaim key terms that have been coopted by Western Modernity. We theorize new terms to shed light on the great varieties of Latinx writing, rhetoric, and literacies that continue to emerge and circulate in the culture at large.

We are motivated, in part, by the writing of Walter Mignolo, from whom we borrow the epistemic delinking concept. That term, itself adapted by Mignolo from Anibal Quijano, describes a process by which "other principles of knowledge and understanding" emerge from the colonized background in order to clear space for decolonial approaches to ethics and politics (453). Epistemic delinking helps establish a separate conceptual space for "thinking otherwise"; that is, for thinking of writing, literacy, and discourse apart from traditional (i.e., Greco-Roman) histories and theories of rhetoric and apart from traditional (i.e., classical, liberal) notions of race and ethnicity.

We are motivated as well by the fact that, as teachers of writing, we work in spaces where rhetoric, education, and culture overlap and intertwine. Precisely as Latinxs, we believe we have especially valuable (though not necessarily privileged) perspectives on these spaces. Moreover, we think such perspectives are tuned to the current historical moment, in which Latinx communities across the United States find themselves on the verge of acquiring transformative cultural and political power. In addition, we believe that as the country's demographics continue to change, our field will feel more urgently the need to recognize, theorize, and teach the intersections of writing, pedagogy, and politics.

We are aware of keyword scholarship that has been written in the field. Notably, the work of Paul Heilker and Peter Vandenberg's *Keywords in Composition Studies* and their more recent *Keywords in Writing Studies* offers something of a parallel narrative to our project. Although our project's substance is different, we nonetheless see it as a fellow traveler of these books, which also seek not only to pin terms down for a while but also to illustrate the richness of the available vocabularies for thinking about writing and rhetoric. Our difference is that we seek, through our examinations of keywords, to work our way into ongoing discussions, and to open up possibilities for new ones, particularly when these discussions—old or new—stand to affect Latinx students and scholars of composition.

Another inspiration for the collection is Raymond Williams's *Keywords: A Vocabulary of Culture and Society*. In his introduction to that book, Williams explains that an "officialized" common language—codified, for example, in the *Oxford English Dictionary*—should not stigmatize outsider groups from using language in unique and culturally specific but unofficial ways. His project was not intended as "a neutral review of meanings" (21). Rather, he wanted to explore "a vocabulary of a crucial area of social and cultural discussion" for contemporary use (21). Williams was less interested in transmitting an already-established culture than in examining the terms with which culture is—and continues to be—understood, defined, and imagined. Doing so, he believed, would put people in a better position to establish "a vocabulary to use to find our own ways in, to change as we find it necessary to change it, as we go on making our own language and history" (22).

In our context, at this moment in history, we hope to do something similar. We examine the keywords in order to create a more inclusive "official" vocabulary, to represent the perspectives of an "outsider" group of Latinx scholars who are nonetheless familiar with the "insider" discourses of Composition and Rhetoric and with decolonial theory. Of course, our project's context is different from Williams's. We want to pursue the possibilities of a decolonial approach to our particular field, to rethink and redefine terms relevant to Composition and Rhetoric by virtue of their role in promoting either oppression or liberation. As such, and following Mignolo, our task is to be epistemically disobedient not only with regard to our terms but also with regard to the field itself.

Even though this project deals with terms and their variable meanings, we do not intend to privilege theory at the expense of materialities. Despite being academics and thereby enjoying the privilege of being able to live, to some extent, "the life of the mind," we do not think we can afford to remain intellectually cloistered. This is because the Western Modernity that Mignolo and others have documented is still at work assimilating and consuming. Dispossession and displacement have not ended with Civil Rights gains and nominal equality. The harmful rhetoric of color-blindness is still blinding many to the material realities of twenty-first century life for many Latinxs. Incidents of racism, often deadly, are continually visited on the colored poor. Furthermore, sovereign nations are still dispossessed and exploited, their sacred lands stolen. Acknowledging these continued threats must be another part of this critical project. We believe that by changing and owning these critical terms, we can begin to clear a path toward positive change. We shine a light on the ongoing threats posed by epistemic colonialism—what Mignolo calls *coloniality*—and the material consequences that it underwrites.

Coloniality and its counterpart, decoloniality, are particularly important terms in this book because they admit a wide range of intellectual, cultural, and historical concerns. As Eve Tuck and K. Wayne Yang forcefully note, the term *decolonization* is often used (inaccurately, as they see it) to describe a range of gestures and actions one might take against the continuing hegemony of European-based culture and epistemology. Such gestures often "make no mention of Indigenous peoples...or the contributions of Indigenous intellectuals and activists to theories and frameworks of decolonization" (2–3). Furthermore, Tuck and Yang note that "there is often little recognition given to the immediate context of settler colonialism" on which such gestures—made at conferences across the United States on soil that once belonged to indigenous people—are made (2–3).

This bitter irony serves as a reminder that decolonization has a material meaning, one that refers quite literally to abandoning the colony—to leaving, or being made to leave land that you settled. The chapters in this book thus acknowledge the problematics of decolonization, and whereas the term may appear in its metaphorical or epistemological form in some of the pages that follow, we adhere to the spirit of Tuck and Yang's critique. But because we work with, on, and in language, we must be attuned to the dynamics of signification, figuration, and metaphor, as well as their material effects.

Other Composition and Rhetoric scholars have already begun the process of recreating, redefining, and reviving. For example, Damián Baca's and Victor Villanueva's edited collection, *Rhetorics of the Americas*, works toward new understandings of rhetoric by looking back to pre-Conquest, Mesoamerican writing systems. The essays in that book pay attention to missing voices and examine rhetorical practices associated with indigenous cultures of this hemisphere—cultures that, until relatively recently, were thought by scholars and intellectuals not to possess levels of literacy comparable to those of the West. *Rhetorics of the Americas* has thus helped begin the work of delinking "the" history of rhetoric from the European (specifically, the Greek and Roman) origins to which it has been habitually and reflexively tethered.

And since the idea of rhetoric has intellectually underwritten the field of composition for decades, any such shifts in the former must have consequences for the latter. It is possible to see the current project, then, as one such consequence. We mean to expand the intellectual parameters of the field, not only to benefit Latinxs and other students and scholars of color, but also to expand the horizons of all involved in Composition Studies. Delinking is for everyone.

This book is divided into four parts. In Part I, "Basics," Chaps. 1, 2, and 3 provide a framework for critically understanding how color and language intersect in both traditional and nontraditional intellectual spaces, and they challenge traditional multicultural approaches to curricula, pedagogy, scholarship, and policy. Iris Ruiz explores the concept of "race" in Chap. 1 from a critical historical perspective, beginning with the sixteenth century, to show how current discussions of racism in the US oversimplify the issue, thus preventing its careful examination and even legitimating race as a concept.

Steven Alvarez describes a shift, in the Americas, in Chap. 2 from literacy models that treat reading and writing as autonomous and ahistorical skills to models that see all forms of communication as situated and context-dependent. While drawing on Mignolo's interdisciplinary study of hemispheric literacy stretched geographically and politically across the so-called New World, Alvarez also acknowledges the work of Damián Baca and Victor Villanueva for advancing studies of transnational literacies. However, he argues that further cross-field collaboration is necessary in the Americas. Alvarez claims that the newer contextual approaches to literacy open spaces for translingual diversity and critical literacy that can account for how colonial power has legislated language and language use.

Ana Milena Ribero challenges the very idea of a "citizen" in Chap. 3, and she examines how DREAMers may consider themselves to be of the United States culturally, even when legal definitions of citizenship will not account for them. Ribero argues that despite more humane and subtle theorizations of citizenship, the concept remains essentially exclusionary, as it is based on racialized, gendered, and sexualized notions of belonging.[2] Arguing that because citizenship is always already exclusionary, therefore incapable of being fully decolonized, Ribero contends that decolonial imaginings must work instead to envision the end of citizenship as a rights-bearing state of being.

Part II, "Making Texts", problematizes our assumptions about composing texts, including those notions that consider text production to be a process of composing seamless narratives with stable or static meanings. José M. Cortez offers a pointed critique of decolonial thinking and scholarship in Chap. 4 through his examination of history, or historiography. Specifically, he questions the ability of critical historiography to delink from the pervasive influence of Eurocentrism. More important, he suggests that the very desire to delink is itself a symptom of that Eurocentrism.

Similarly, in Chap. 5 José Luis Cano claims that code-switching hides its own colonialism by treating language as an evolving phenomenon rather than something over which groups struggle. To fully consider Latinx rhetorical practices in a decolonial context, Cano employs Juan C. Guerra's concept of code-segregation to explore which aspects of code-switching might be reconsidered in order for Latinxs to reclaim their own rhetorical practices. According to Cano, full bilingualism and fully bilingual Latinxs should be the point of departure for literacy, particularly writing.

In Chap. 6 Raúl Sánchez asks theoretical questions about the nature and function of writing that arise in the wake of two intellectual developments emerging from Latin America and Latin American Studies: the recognition that Mesoamerican communication systems are writing systems on a rhetorical par with those of Western Modernity, and the attempt to establish epistemological spaces that are somehow delinked from that same Western Modernity. Juxtaposing Mignolo's decoloniality and Jacques Derrida's deconstruction, Sánchez looks forward to the prospect of a genuinely comparative approach to the study of writing and rhetoric.

Part III, "Self-(Re)Definitions," captures some particulars of Latinxs' experiences in the United States. These terms are cultural but also political in that they signal resistance against complete assimilation. They keep personal and cultural histories alive through their specific ties to Latinx cultural practices and indigenous history. Cruz Medina's Chap. 7, "Pocho," follows Damián Baca's call to explore the contemporary influence of Mesoamerican languages and rhetorical traditions. He points to the term's Nahuatl root to show how current identity tropes can function as decolonizing language strategies, exposing new ways of knowing and providing new modes of resistance. In delinking the term from its associations with cultural treason, Medina exposes the colonialism implicit in its history as an accusation or epithet. He then examines how the term is currently negotiated in online environments by digital-age Latinxs.

In Chap. 8 Gabriela Raquel Ríos highlights an ongoing debate about the decolonial and/or liberatory potential of *mestizaje* from the disciplinary perspectives of Latin American, Chicanx, and Indigenous Studies. She explores the limits of the term as yet another identifying marker rooted in colonial practice. For Octavio Pimentel and Nancy Wilson in Chap. 9, *éxito* and related terms signal a cultural value system oriented toward collectivity—one that is often at odds with the dominant US value system, which stresses individualism. Pimentel and Wilson explore the conflict between these systems, and they argue for greater alignment between the collectivist goals of many Latinxs' home cultures and the goals of the educational institutions that are supposed to serve them. Finally in Chap. 10, Candace K. Zepeda's Chicana Feminism articulates what Chela Sandoval calls a "theory of difference" in order to bring issues of gender, race, culture, and class to bear on theories of spatiality, specifically Edward Soja's concept of the Third Space.

Finally, Part IV is titled Political Rhetoric, and although all of the terms in this book are political (or have political dimensions), those in this part are acutely and perhaps more directly so. The authors of the two chapters provide insights into how Latinxs are seen by others, particularly in the dominant US culture. Amanda Espinosa-Aguilar explores the politics of fear behind the term *illegal* in Chap. 11. Looking at how it and related terms are deployed to advance regressive anti-Latinx legislative and political agendas, she contends that the idea is to create "unsubstantiated fears in the minds of privileged voters." Similarly, for Marcos del Hierro, in Chap. 12 the label *mojado* stamps illegitimate sociopolitical status onto US brown bodies regardless of their citizenship status. He explains that what began as a pejorative term for poor migrant workers extends to all Latinxs crossing national, social, professional, and political borders—a continuation of coloniality and white supremacy.

In the end, a decolonial approach to disciplinary discourses (and their attendant keywords) must reflect a profoundly multi- or transcultural, multi- or translingual world. It must recognize that Western knowledge and skills will not be adequate to resolve contemporary issues, certainly not those faced by contemporary indigenous people and those others who experience daily (to borrow the title of a Mignolo book) "the darker side" of Western Modernity. With this in mind, we offer the terms in this book, delinked from their usual contexts and linked to new ones, and offering respect for the variety of knowledge that circulates among us, often without acknowledgment.

WORKS CITED

Baca, Damián, and Victor Villanueva, eds. *Rhetorics of the Americas: 3114 BCE to 2012 CE*. New York: Palgrave, 2012.

Heilker, Paul, and Peter Vandenberg, eds. *Keywords in Composition Studies*. Portsmouth, NH: Boynton/Cook, 1996.

Heilker, Paul, and Peter Vandenberg, eds. *Keywords in Writing Studies*. Logan, UT: Utah State University Press, 2015.

Mignolo, Walter D. Delinking: The Rhetoric of Modernity, the Logic of Coloniality and the Grammar of De-coloniality. *Cultural Studies* 21 (2007): 449–514.

Tuck, Eve, and K. Wayne Wang. Decolonization is Not a Metaphor. *Decolonization: Indigeneity, Education & Society* 1 (2012): 1–40.

Williams, Raymond. *Keywords: A Vocabulary of Culture and Society*. New York: Oxford University Press, 1976.

Iris D. Ruiz
Raúl Sánchez

PART I

Basics

CHAPTER 1

Race

Iris D. Ruiz

INTRODUCTION: RACE TO THE SURFACE

Race. It's a taboo word. Mention it in a classroom setting, and opinions start fluctuating along a continuum of race-based views and beliefs such as "All Lives Matter" or "Black Lives Matter" as if these two are in opposition to one another. Yet, one wonders, how can they be in opposition to one another when recent instances of numerous murders by police have been inflicted upon innocent, unarmed black men in the U.S, demonstrating that all lives do not matter because black lives do not seem matter? While the above example highlights a very recent moment in which this book has been published, race has been a topic of great controversy and heartache. W.E.B. Du Bois, recently credited with being the first African-American sociologist, had a tacit understanding of this complicated term as he devoted much of his scholarship to the phenomenon of race in the late nineteenth and early twentieth century, a time when race was a very prominently seen phenomenon in our country. We are now over a century removed from Jim Crow racial segregation laws in which Du Bois was writing and theorizing about race and the "Negro Problem",

I. D. Ruiz (✉)
Merritt Writing Program, University of California, Merced, Merced, CA, USA

© The Editor(s) (if applicable) and The Author(s) 2016   3
I.D. Ruiz, R. Sánchez (eds.), *Decolonizing Rhetoric and Composition Studies*, DOI 10.1057/978-1-137-52724-0_1

and, here we are, still trying to make the case for why we still need to talk about race. Du Bois suggests that race is, "a group of contradictory forces, facts, and tendencies" and not an actual noun.

As Dubois points out in much of his work, due the solidification of race as a marker of inferiority and social position in colonial societies, the words *race* and *racial* have often been approached haphazardly or simplistically with little to no historical context, especially by hate groups such as the Aryan Nation whose members identify themselves as racial purists. As a result of decontextualized and simplistic conversations about race, great schisms in communicative and interpretive practices occur and dialogue shuts down. The schisms, I argue, necessitate the continuation of taboo-laden race discussions.

Diversity in populations where difficult conversations might take place does not remove the taboo—race is a challenging topic for people everywhere. I teach at the second most diverse campus of the University of California: UC Merced, which is a Hispanic-Serving Institution, with a student population that is more than 45 % "Hispanic" or Latinx. Nevertheless, students have not always shown an interest in the topic of race. Having taught in less diverse environments, such as UC San Diego, I'm quite aware of how student demographics can affect pedagogy. In the case of UCSD, however, the student demographics correlated with the desire to engage in the topic of race: white students were more reluctant to engage in the topic whereas students of color who were non-Asians discussed it eagerly.

Given these experiences, I've learned that regardless of student demographics encountered over the past 15 years of teaching first-year composition, does not automatically correlte with whether or not students welcome the opportunity to engage in the topic of race—no matter where their hometown is, how they look, sound, or write. This is true regardless of whether the discussions are grounded in sociological approaches to the study of race, such as those forwarded by W.E.B. Du Bois and Booker T. Washington; or linguistic theories, such as sociolinguistics, who make connections between language and race; or even in textual analysis of "objective historical texts" such as Charles Darwin's *Origin of Species.*

In short, "race" is difficult to discuss, as it entails difficult and numerous political nuances and many unlearned, unknown, and silenced histories. If the many nuances of race are not approached from an equally complex attitude, the implications on future race relations will evolve in a more segregationist manner based on simplistic, colonial, and decontextualized considerations of current race relations.

Race as the "Still" Absent Presence in Composition Studies: A Critical Historical Treatment of Race

On the particular question of *race*, the field of composition and rhetoric also has struggled. For example, in 1968 an issue of *College Composition and Communication* acknowledged Dr. Martin Luther King, Jr.'s assassination and that act's significance, and it noted the field's failure to address the question of race. The *CCC* editor at the time, William F. Irmscher, hoped to "open channels of communication we do not now have" (105). But Ernece B. Kelly was less optimistic, noting "the awful resistance of white participants [at the 1968 CCCC Convention] to the challenges to recognize their biases and to work to defeat them" (107). Almost 60 years later, we can see how right she was to be wary.

Those who are and have been devoted to keeping questions of race alive in the field have shown that while there might have been honest attempts—now and then—to deal with the term *race*, in the long run, composition and rhetoric has effectively replaced this important term with less-threatening euphemisms such as *diversity* and *underrepresentation*. On a similar note, the language of race and racism is regulated by mainstream publications in Composition Studies. That regulation organizes learning in educational settings like the writing classroom, while shaping how Composition Studies practitioners discuss race in scholarly and pedagogical settings, both of which have profound impacts on everyday social interactions outside of educational settings. One compelling critique of this problem was offered by Jennifer Clary-Lemon in her *CCC* article, "The Racialization of Composition Studies: Scholarly Rhetoric of Race since 1990." Examining the language of College Composition and Communication and College English since 1990, she discovered that the majority of race-related work published in these journals rarely uses the words "race or racism." Instead, their authors utilize vague metaphors such "diversity, inclusion, and social justice" when alluding to racialized phenomena (W6). This metonymic slide has caused potentially productive discussions about race to lose their precision. In short, the field has not addressed racism in all of its complexities. We still need to talk about race, as it is still the "absent presence" (Prendergast 36).

In an attempt to open up a critical dialogue abour race, this chapter offers a noncomprehensive but critical and historical treatment of race. It does so while problematizing three of its definitions from a decolonial perspective. Through this lens, this chapter attempts to delink the term *race* from its historical ties to Western hierarchies. Attempting to provide a contested, decolonial consideration of race and connect its colonial roots to the twenty-first century dilemma of the great racial divide, I demonstrate one possible thread as a discursive act of what Walter Mignolo calls "epistemic disobedience." I attempt to delink race from its religious, scientific, and discursive points of origin. Through considering each point, this chapter shows how the first two points are limited and continue to divide people in a manner that privileges groups of people who produce, disseminate, and legitimize such discourses. The third point, however, offers possibilities to disrupt these limitations.

Given all the points of origin explored here, the chapter suggests a more well-rounded view of race that can lead to peaceful, humane, and productive discussions about both race and racism in decolonial, pedagogical, and personal spaces. *Decolonial* theory posits that no single vantage point gives one group or culture the capacity to claim biological, religious, or social superiority over another group or culture. Instead, decoloniality operates from a respect for various historical trajectories while acknowledging that racial identity, and therefore racism, produces real, material, but malleable, consequences. The chapter concludes with a consideration of Critical Race Theory as one possible decolonial pedagogical practice that tries to delink legal discourse, in particular, from claims of race neutrality.

RELIGION

From the beginning, racism has been a problem—the problem—in the United States. We have seen the cruelest behaviors exhibited toward others because of their skin color. If we were to ask why, we might be at a loss. Nonetheless, those of us who study the origins, uses, and effects of language know that language itself plays a major role in division and classification and, thus, the treatment of subjects, including human beings. Language produces real, material consequences that go beyond human instinct and that can even determine human instinct. To *hate*, for example, might be a human instinct, but that does not mean it is necessarily instinctual to hate a particular group because of physical differences. If language produces material consequences in the shaping of reality, then racism can be understood as a linguistically taught behavior. Still the question remains: Where does racism come from and why do we identify races of people? This section begins with a look back to the sixteenth century.

In "Epistemic Disobedience, Independent Thought and De-Colonial Freedom," Mignolo indicates the partial fictions that accompany any legitimized, academic explanation for the rise of science and modernity—and, ultimately, of racism: "Once upon a time scholars assumed that the knowing subject in the disciplines is transparent, disincorporated from the known and untouched by the geo-political configuration of the world in which people are racially ranked and regions are racially configured" (2). Here, Mignolo makes a connection—although one of disconnection—between *modernity* and *race*. Following Mignolo, this chapter posits that once upon a time, the world order was changing due to expansion, conquests, annihilation, and colonial pursuits. These events, which seemed natural, unproblematic, and even justifiable, were rhetorically framed as objective, benevolent behaviors.

As we know, however, such events were unwelcome impositions on the cultures, lands, and religions of what are now called the Americas. A clash of cultures took place—and continues to take place—between the colonized and colonizers. For example, in *Aztec Thought and Culture: A Study of the Ancient Nahuatl Mind*, Miguel León-Portilla provides evidence that during the Spanish Conquest, verbal exchanges between *tlamatinime* (indigenous spiritual leaders) and Spanish missionaries reflected unwelcome intrusions and the silencing of indigenous knowledge. These exchanges point to the beginning of racism against brown and, soon after, black people during the sixteenth century in what would eventually be called Latin America.

In those verbal, poetic exchanges, the *tlamatinime* exhibited an awareness of being rhetorically manipulated in order to benefit from European colonial projects that exploited and destroyed indigenous land and culture. The indigenous were regarded as barbarians, and their religion, worldview, and authority were ignored. Mignolo notes that the idea of the "barbarian" was "taken from the Greek language and historical experience" and came to serve sixteenth-century capitalist interests when "Christianity … affirmed its complicity with capitalism" ("Delinking" 471).

Referring to the *Apologética Historia Sumaria*, written by Dominican Friar Bartolomae de las Casas, Mignolo mentions the types of barbarians classified by las Casas, all of whom reflected "*babarie* negative" (negative barbarianism). Mignolo argues that the barbarian trope was becoming part of the Western narrative of modernity, reemerging "as Western Christians in Latin and vernacular Western languages began to construct a narrative of themselves." In contrast to these Christians, he writes, "'barbarians' were those who lacked something in the area of … alphabetic writing because they lived in a state of nature" ("Delinking" 471).

As European colonies spread across the globe, their inhabitants viewed Christianity as the only true and right religion while simultaneously negating indigenous religion by discrediting its precepts. Portillo's critical analysis of European–indigenous exchanges identifies the connection between las Casas's understanding of barbarism and indigenous religion when he "identified oppositional barbarians as enemies of Christianity, those who envied it and wanted to destroy it" ("Delinking" 471). The oppositional barbarians las Casas was referring to were brown.

With these colonial processes underway, European colonizers saw nature as something to be used for material gain. As such, nature was integral to the early stages of capitalist development and global exchange. Cultures without alphabetic writing systems were considered incapable of understanding the vast potential of their natural resources. (Here, we start to get a glimpse of the racial differences in intelligence levels that became more popular during the eighteenth century.) Alphabetic languages were the hallmarks of more civilized and more advanced people who possessed and used them to manipulate nature.

Along with the view that barbarians were inferior and in need of "development" came the idea that their religions were less developed, more pagan, and even evil, especially if they practiced blood sacrifice and polytheism. However, in *The Colloquies* by Bernardino de Sahagún, it is evident that the *tlamatinime* publicly defended the Nahuatl religion and understood that the idea of polytheism was a Western concept imposed on them with little regard for their own theology, which refers to a belief in one god. It also is apparent that the indigenous held a clear and rational basis for their way of life. Consider this translated excerpt (León-Portilla 64):

> *You said*
> *that we know not*
> *the Lord of the Close Vicinity,*
> *to Whom the heavens and the earth belong*
> *You said*
> *That our gods are not true gods.*
> *that you speak;*
> *because of them we are disturbed*
> *because of them we are troubled*
> *For our ancestors*
> *before us, who lived upon the earth,*
> *were unaccustomed to speak thus.*
> *From them have we inherited*
> *our pattern of life*
> *which in truth did they hold . . .*
> *We know*

on Whom life is dependent;
on Whom the perpetuation of the race depends.

This excerpt challenges the concept of inherent inferiority based on Christian justifications, which dismiss indigenous logic and cultural practices—often to appropriate them later for capitalist ventures, as Mignolo and others have pointed out ("Delinking" 462).

Furthermore, the silencing of the indigenous, Aztec *tlamatinime* becomes apparent as they were aware of their demise and that their god, proclaimed to be false, was being taken from them. As the excerpt also demonstrates, the Aztec *tlamatinime* knew of the inherent connection between the survival of their religious beliefs and the continuation of their race. Note, however, that the idea of race is tied to their religious practices, not their skin color. As a gesture toward "race" continuation then, the *tlamatinime* continued to defend their beliefs although they knew that their race was being destroyed due to their "wrong" religion—their race.

This historical account challenges current conceptions of race and shows how the geopolitical and colonial matrix of power operated to attach the word *race* to color through the debasement of indigenous religion. At this time, only one religion (race) counted: Christianity (Europeans). One's religion was considered to be one's race until "race" became associated with the "wrong" race attached to one's color (brown). From this point on, color also was tied to race (religion). Due to this contortion, racism toward brown people and images of them as barbarians, to some extent, still exists. The power of Christian discourse currently is matched only by what we see in efforts to spread democratic principles tied to US Christian doctrines, which are now embraced by many races (colors of people).

SCIENCE

When religious rhetoric no longer provided legitimate explanations for discriminating against people of color or other races, scientism and appeals to a perverse form of rationality gained notoriety (Hudson). According to Jürgen Habermas, Hegel's notion of modernity breaks with religious doctrine on the notion of individual subjectivity; he notes:

[T]he principle of subjectivity determines the forms of modern culture. This holds true first of all for objectifying science, which disenchants nature at the same time that it liberates the knowing subject. "Thus [writes Hegel], all miracles were disallowed: for nature was a now system of known and recognized laws; man is at home in it, and only that remains standing in which he is at home; he is free through the acquaintance he has gained with 'nature.'" (17)

But with this "disenchantment" of nature and the "liberation" of the subject came, eventually, ideas of genetic superiority, which were used to justify the supposedly natural order of racial classification schemes. With the barrage of global exchanges of raw goods, and the rise of capitalism and science, racial rankings thus became "scientific" instead of religious. Race became a supposedly disinterested representation of real genetic differences, sparking the eugenics movement of the late nineteenth century, which attributed one's social position in life to biological differences such as inferior intellectual capacities.

Although eugenics can be traced as far back as Plato's *Republic*, it gained legitimacy in the United States in the late nineteenth and early twentieth centuries, particularly in the Ivy League—some of whose scholars promoted the idea of a superior genetic race through natural selection or selective breeding. In *The Blood of the Nation: A Study of the Decay of Races through the Survival of the Unfit*, biologist and Stanford University's founding president David Starr Jordan, "scientifically" concluded that human qualities and conditions, such as talent and poverty, were passed through heredity. As a Harvard graduate student during this time, W.E.B. Du Bois also supported a form of eugenics, which in some measure lurks behind his notion of the Talented Tenth.[1]

One may wonder why an African American would contemplate such a theory, especially during the time of Jim Crow. Du Bois himself seems to acknowledge, indirectly, the oddity of it. Writing later in his life, he notes that the history of "the race concept" to which he had devoted his life contains "all sorts of illogical trends and irreconcilable tendencies." Eventually, he decided that race might not be a concept at all but rather, as, "a group of contradictory forces, facts and tendencies" (*Dusk of Dawn* 67).

Eventually, as Mignolo points out, nineteenth-century eugenics-based arguments for racial separation and for fostering a better race took hold in South America and "returned as a boomerang to Europe in the Holocaust" ("Epistemic" 16). Atrocities on both sides of the Atlantic, then, justify an attempt to delink from—not simply to decry—Western racial classification systems. Mignolo defines delinking as a "double movement." One step is to unveil "the geo-political location" of Western epistemology, which pretends to have no location. The other step, taken simultaneously, was to affirm "the modes and principles of knowledge that have been denied by the rhetoric of Christianization, civilization, progress, development, market democracy" and racial superiority ("Delinking" 463).

Mignolo's double movement, in some sense, mirrors DuBois's double-consciousness. Du Bois understood and articulated what it meant to have a "black" worldview that was not inherently inferior but that was economically and racially oppressed due to unnatural, pseudo-scientifically based codification systems.

RACE AS A SOCIAL INSTRUMENT

According to Mignolo, Michel Foucault's key concept of biopolitics "refers to emerging state technologies (strategies, in a more traditional vocabulary) of population control that went hand in hand with the emergence of the modern nation-state" ("Epistemic" 16). Through this concept, Foucault presents an important analysis of race as an instrument of domination. Identifying racism as "the basic mechanism of power," he then defines it at length (*Society* 254: 254–255). For Foucault, racism is

> . . . primarily a way of introducing a break into the domain of life that is under power's control: the break between what must live and what must die. The appearance within the biological continuum of the human race of races, the distinction among races, the hierarchy of races, the fact that certain races are described as good and that others, in contrast, are described as inferior: all this is a way of fragmenting the field of the biological that power controls. It is a way of separating out the groups that exist within a population. It is, in short, a way of establishing a biological-type caesura within a population that appears to be a biological domain. This will allow power to treat that population as a mixture of races, or to be more accurate, to treat the species, to subdivide the species it controls, into the subspecies known, precisely, as races.

Mignolo notes that even though Foucault limited his analysis to Europe, such technologies or strategies became popular in Latin America as well: "In Argentina (and South America in general), for example, the push for eugenics toward the end of the 19th century has been studied in detail lately" (16).

Citing Foucault, Linda Brodkey sees the human body as "the irreducible element," that "functions as our most fundamental cite of power in our struggles against the forces of socialization, repression, and punishment" (273). In this context, she finds it impossible to see language as a disinterested reflection of reality. Brodkey explains why she leans toward post-structural theories of discourse, "the structural argument concerning the arbitrary or neutral relationship between language and reality is an account of linguistic structural variation." It does not "attempt to describe and explain the structure of the social, political, and historical circumstances under which people think and write." More to the point, Brodkey argues:

> [W]hile it may be true that the linguistic marking of "woman" and "black" in such familiar binary pairs as "man and woman" and "black and white" is arbitrary or neutral, I doubt whether many women or black people live in a world where the logic of linguistic markedness overrides the logic of, say, institutional racism and sexism. (9)

In short, racist conditions of society are reflected in language and discourse, which challenges theoretical and apolitical notions of linguistic arbitrariness corralated with the work of Saussure.

Moving from language to a discourse, James Berlin has argued that current-traditional rhetoric espouses such an acontextual view of language. In addition, current traditional rhetoric is closely associated with scientism and this view of discourse is related to the rise of eugenics movement. He says common definitions of current traditional rhetoric hold that "knowledge in all areas of human behavior [can] be readily discovered and validated through scientific method" (37). In contrast to this narrow view of discourse, Berlin argues that social environment affects how one understands and engages with discourse and language, which in turn affect that environment even while representing it. If this is the case, and if Brodkey and Foucault are right, then race is entirely discursive, and it is understood and discussed through social communicative processes created by and for dominant classes (or what Foucault would vaguely refer to as "power").

For most undergraduate students, the idea of race and reality as discursively constructed is too much to swallow quickly, so the task of teaching must be handled with care. For me, it is helpful to consider Brodkey's discussion of resistance as a "necessary illusion" that one adopts in order "to believe that social change is possible" and in order to believe in "the possibility of shifting discursive positions and [in] articulating positive representations of oneself [as] a more effective, a more inclusive and lasting, form of political resistance than either silence or violence" (23). It is also helpful to note that, in Spanish, the word *ilusión* signifies not only error and deception but also excitement.

If racism is a discursive illusion (in the negative sense), it still manages to produce very real consequences. One solution is to break it with another illusion (in the positive sense) that identifies and refuses fixed racial hierarchies communicated through language. To embrace this position, however, one first has to agree that the current illusion of race exists, that it exists as a *negative* illusion, and that it has thus cast a shadow on people's ideas of civility, morality, and equality. It is the reason why #blacklivesmatter and the Dream Act exist. The illusion is powerful, but it can change. Structures can be torn down and rebuilt to reflect new ideas and philosophies surrounding human relations regardless of one's race (color). One only has to look at #blacklivesmatter and the events in Ferguson, Baltimore, New York, and elsewhere to see the growing national consciousness that is trying to change the current structure of racial inequality.

Delinking Through Critical Race Theory

Critical Race Theory (CRT) is a type of decolonizing knowledge, which Mignolo describes as questioning an allegedly objective body of knowledge. CRT and decolonial theory have similar goals but operate from difference places. To perform CRT is to enact a type of epistemic disobedience that questions legal discourse's validity, particularly with regard to its supposed lack of interest and "color-blind" rhetoric. As such, CRT breaks the silence of a normalized discourse that has historically been used as a means of oppression against racial minorities in the United States.

CRT is useful, for example, in examining cases such as Plessy *vs.* Ferguson, which in 1898 legalized nationwide segregation on the basis of the now-discredited "separate but equal" doctrine. At the time, however, this doctrine was thought not to violate the Constitution because it provided for equality, albeit separately. Looking back on this case from a CRT perspective, one might ask: Who were the advocates and beneficiaries of segregation, and what were their underlying motives? In addition, we might look into the backgrounds of the judges presiding over this case.

The state's legal brief, for example, was prepared personally by Attorney General Milton Joseph Cunningham of Natchitoches and New Orleans. Earlier, Cunningham had fought to restore white supremacy during Reconstruction. Louisiana Justice Edward Douglass White was one of the majority: He was a member of the New Orleans Pickwick Club and the Crescent City White League; the latter was a paramilitary organization that had supported white supremacy with violence throughout the 1870s in an effort to suppress black voting and regain political power for white property owners. These underlying circumstances directly challenges the approach to legal discourse that considers legal decisions to be the result of disinterested interpretations of the law. The law, the outcome of this case, and the language that upheld it obscured an underlying motive of white supremacy. Exposing the interested nature of the legal discourse, then, is the first step toward eradicating racist legal practices.

Nevertheless, legal practices in the twenty-first century continue to pretend to practice objectivity, keeping them heavily implicated in the colonial matrix of power that oppresses and incarcerates non-Whites at alarming rates. Legal policies claim objectivity and ignore the historical injustices suffered by racial minorities going back generations; the law operates as if all human beings in the United States are—and have been—on an equal footing. In the process of delinking from the colonial matrix of power's legal system, it is easy to become aware of how people of color are convicted of crimes far more often than their white counterparts.[2] Individuals simply should not take for granted class interests, political interests, personal interests, and history.

CONCLUSION

This chapter has provided a partial historical treatment of the term *race* in order to understand various current debates surrounding it in contemporary culture, at a moment when people still stand on the shoulders of the Civil Rights movement, in the still-living memory (50 years) of a time when government policy was—for a brief time—explicitly focused on achieving racial equality. It has considered one possible trajectory to delink race from its colonial framework which operates across religious, scientific, and religious discursive constructs. Racism operates from discursively constructed racial classifications and hierarchies, which serves current power structures, affects material realities unequally across racial groups, and distorts the real-life experiences of humans who belong to races with long histories of oppression. The inequalities that racism creates are inconsistent with the promised pursuit of life, liberty, and the pursuit of happiness for US individuals. So, let's continue to talk about race because as Du Bois's suggests, race is a "group of contradictory forces, facts and tendencies" and race is killing people.

NOTES

1. See Sherman.
2. See Report.

WORKS CITED

Berlin, James A. *Rhetoric and Reality: Writing Instruction in American Colleges, 1900–1985*. Carbondale: Southern Illinois UP, 1987. Print.

Bonilla-Silva, Eduardo. *Racism Without Racists: Color-Blind Racism and the Persistence of Racial Inequality in the United States*. Lanham, MD: Rowman and Littlefield, 2003. Print.

Brodkey, Linda. *Writing Permitted in Designated Areas Only*. Minneapolis: University of Minnesota Press, 1996. Print.

DuBois, W. E. B. *Dusk of Dawn*. Oxford: Oxford UP, 2007 (1940). Print.

Foucault, Michel. *"Society Must Be Defended": Lectures at the College de France, 1975–76*. Eds. Mauro Bertani and Alessandro Fontana and Trans. David Macey. New York: Picador, 1997. Print.

Habermas, Jürgen. *The Philosophical Discourse of Modernity: Twelve Lectures*. Trans. Frederick G. Lawrence. Boston: MIT, 1987. Print.

Irmscher, William F. In Memoriam: Rev. Dr. Martin Luther King, Jr.: 1929–1968. *College Composition and Communication* 19 (1968): 105.

Jordan, David Starr. *The Blood of the Nation: A Study of the Decay of Races through the Survival of the Unfit*. Boston: American Unitarian Organization, 1910. Internet Archive. https://archive.org/details/bloodofnationstu00jorduoft

Kelly, Ernece B. Murder of the American Dream. *College Composition and Communication* 19 (1968): 106–108. Print.

León-Portilla, Miguel. *Aztec Thought and Culture: A Study of the Ancient Nahuatl Mind*. Trans. Jack Emory Davis. Norman, OK: U of Oklahoma P, 1963.

Mauer, Marc. Addressing Racial Disparities in Incarceration. *The Prison Journal* 91, no. 3, Suppl (2011): 87S–101S. http://tpj.sagepub.com/content/91/3_suppl/87S.full.pdf+html

Mignolo, Walter D. Delinking. *Cultural Studies* 21 (2007): 449–514.

Mignolo, Walter D. Epistemic Disobedience, Independent Thought and De-Colonial Freedom. *Theory, Culture & Society* 26, no. 7–8 (2009): 1–23. Web.

Prendergast, Catherine. Race: The Absent Presence in Composition Studies. *College Composition and Communication* 50 (1998): 36–53. Print.

Report of The Sentencing Project to the United Nations Human Rights Committee Regarding Racial Disparities in the United States Criminal Justice System, August 2013. Web. sentencingproject.org

Sherman, Shantella Y. In Search of Purity: Popular Eugenics and Racial Uplift among New Negroes 1915–1935. Dissertation. 2014 Spring. http://digitalcommons.unl.edu/historydiss/68/

CHAPTER 2

Literacy

Steven Alvarez

After the European "discovery" and conquest of the Americas, Western forms of literacy subordinated Amerindian epistemologies and then categorized them according to the invented colonial difference that emerged. European literacies dominated the hemisphere, physically and symbolically destroying Indigenous writing practices deemed as nonliterate at best or demonic at worst. Centuries later these European literacies still dominate, with notions of decontextualized autonomous skillsets framing deficit approaches to language standardization policies (Horner and Lu; Kalman and Street).

Research that challenges autonomous models of language and literacy standardization has turned to how various forms of local literacies historically have been marginalized in a hemisphere largely dominated by Spain, Portugal, England, the Netherlands, France, Russia, and later the United States. Spanish, Portuguese, English, French, and Dutch have been the most powerful European languages to have a lasting impact on the standards for literacy in the Americas, especially in the policing of hybridized forms of each language with local vernaculars. The logic of coloniality— and its accompanying rhetoric that attempts to naturalize "modernity"

S. Alvarez (✉)
Writing, Rhetoric, & Digital Studies, University of Kentucky, Lexington, KY, USA

© The Editor(s) (if applicable) and The Author(s) 2016   17
I.D. Ruiz, R. Sánchez (eds.), *Decolonizing Rhetoric and Composition Studies*, DOI 10.1057/978-1-137-52724-0_2

on those deemed marginal—dictates that language standardization is necessary for market growth and for expanding transnational corporate partnerships. But there is room for transdisciplinary scholarship that counters this colonial logic by locating intersections among composition and rhetoric, literacy, and writing studies. The transdisciplinarity of literacy studies already traverses fields, thus providing a model for other cross-disciplinary methodologies that help counter the rhetoric of modernity with positions that reveal the darker sides of colonization and language standardization.

Transdisciplinary conversations between rhetoric and composition and geopolitics have been few, but one compelling example is Damián Baca's *Mestiz@ Scripts, Digital Migrations, and the Territories of Writing.* Baca's work reminds us that rhetoric exists beyond European traditions, and that delinking from Western models opens spaces for counter-rhetorics that challenge the logic of coloniality in the twenty-first century. Also important in this respect is Baca and Victor Villanueva's groundbreaking edited collection, *Rhetorics of the Americas: 3114 BCE to 2012 CE.* In this book, a group of scholars maps rhetorics of the Western hemisphere that have been hushed, but not silenced, by the logic of coloniality. But even though these works deserve credit for moving rhetoric and composition in this important direction, the field needs further cross-field collaboration.

Building on this work, then, I propose translingual literacy studies as way for our field to join conversations in hemispheric studies that examine how translingual literacies and translanguaging practices in the Americas serve as loci of enunciation available for intersectional analysis. I examine these loci of enunciation for with an eye to composition pedagogy. Currently, positions of power in translocal fields generate webs of discourse that codify language standardization privileging European languages as legitimate markers of literacy. Delinking from such colonialist orientations to a genuinely plurilingual orientation requires us, as language and literacy researchers, to focus on local struggles for language legitimacy across the Americas.

A TRANSLINGUAL COUNTER TO LANGUAGE MINORITIZATION IN THE AMERICAS

In the Americas—from Latinxs in the United States and Canada, to the Mixtec in Mexico, to the Quechua in Peru—is the result of contact between or among asymmetrical forces, often across contemporary national boundaries. Five hundred years after the arrival of Europeans, the rhetoric of modernity and development continues to impose standardization despite its history of structured inequality and development dependency.

Work emerging from hemispheric studies, which calibrates the relationship between cultural identities and national geographies, brings to light discrepancies between dominant notions of literacy and language minoritization. It counters the notion that forms of literacy essentially attach to concrete geopolitical boundaries. Instead, it notes that actual forms of literacy are consistently marked by structural powers operating through boundaries to maintain and enforce (di)vision between dominant and minoritized groups. To do this work, hemispheric studies invokes fields such as Latin American/Inter-American studies, ethnic and critical race studies, area studies, migration studies, transnational studies, and postcolonial studies.

Literacy and Numeracy in Latin America, by Brian Street and Judy Kalman, offers insight into how transdisciplinary research across national contexts informs future avenues for collaboration among literacy scholars who are researching language standardization and local ways with words. For methodological knowledge to develop, intersectional transdisciplinary collaboration must take place among a number of fields within the hemispheric studies project. This knowledge will be constantly revised and enriched by research that focuses on transnational narratives of movement, directionalities, positions, social fields, and networks of geopolitical difference. For its part, literacy studies research has demonstrated that a translingual orientation to language acknowledges the repertoires of agents communicating in everyday plurilingual contexts and situations. Translingual orientations treat plurilingualism as the norm and thus recalibrate studies of literacies for intersectional approaches from translocals' views and practices.

Translingual literacy studies aims to contribute to a necessary shift in literacy studies by treating heterogeneity in contact zones as the norm rather than the exception. According to A. Suresh Canagarajah, openness to difference and awareness makes translingual literacies intrinsically rhetorical. Translingual literacies acknowledge ethical values associated with pluralism and power and the suitability of negotiating differences and navigating strategies of reception and interpretation. The rhetorical dimension of translingual literacies allows it to consider communicative competence as not restricted to predefined meanings within individual languages. Rather, it is able to shuttle across diverse language resources in situated interactions, seeing uncertainty and openness as essential to any study of communication and difference. From a hemispheric perspective, the contact zones of translingual literacies undermine monolingual orientations that arbitrarily assume linguistic borders (and structured inequalities) among languages.

For Canagarajah, translingual literacies challenge monolingual assumptions that permeate language education policies. They question orientations that inaccurately depict the brain as being composed of several monolinguals rather than as one plurilingual mind negotiating from a single but varied repertoire of linguistic aptitudes. A translingual orientation embraces social practices that recognize complete language repertoires as resources and that do not perceive any language activity as a learning obstacle.

Delinking from Standardized Languages and Literacies in the Americas

In order to create transformative educational experiences that give students theoretical tools for foregrounding social justice, it is necessary to first delink from the colonial logic of dispossession. According to Walter Mignolo, delinking is a "de-colonial epistemic shift leading to ... pluriversality as a universal project" ("Delinking" 453). Delinking analyzes the politico-economic relationships between the center and the periphery in the colonial matrix of power, between what is deemed standard and what is deemed nonstandard (455). It also informs strategies that disrupt networks of power imbalances, which almost always favor the (colonial) center. Delinking projects seek emancipation from colonial and neo-colonial elites and liberation for the colonized majority in the Americas.

Counter-movements seek to delink through subversive strategies that speak for pluralities and social justice. In particular, education can help transform the socio-material conditions of existence, and it has ties to a history of literacy for liberation in the Americas. What colonial and neo-colonial forces code as nonstandard or illiterate, the colonized in turn read as the continuing legacy of invasion and dispossession, as well as neoliberal values of austerity and privatization. In the context of Mexico, for example, Gregorio Hernandez-Zamora recognizes the power of local literacies responding to imposed global standards that silence local intelligence:

The economic, social and educational problems of people whose lives have proceeded for generations under material and cultural oppression cannot be explained away by the "poor literacy skills" of their individual members, as agencies like the World Bank or OECD would have us believe. Poor literacy and school failure are not individual phenomena in the ex-colonial world, but rather the historical and pervasive result of invasions, slavery and modern "development policies" that, like social winds, respectively push forward or inhibit learning and growth possibilities. (3)

Under the rhetoric of individual growth and economic development, the individual "grows" to become even more "flexible" during times of economic contraction, when conditions become most precarious for the marginalized. In other words, development is simply the dark underside of coloniality. It requires a counter-rhetoric that contests the policing power of such colonialist and neo-colonialist practices as language standardization.

The logic of coloniality manifests itself in a system of economic dependency, which creates the conditions for both austerity of first world countries and global banks over less developed countries and, ironically, at the same time, liberation from oppressive, anti-democratic governments which often give way when entering into the global economy. With their entrance into the global economy, the Americas have borrowed heavily from the World Bank to support and maintain their educational institutions. The United Nations's research into literacy programs across the globe, for example, finds that the external debt for education in the Americas has remained constant:

[I]n 1999–2005 World Bank's loans for education totaled US$400 million, more than half of World Bank loans for education in all regions of the world. Since 1999, five countries—Bolivia, Guyana, Haiti, Honduras and Nicaragua—were integrated to the Heavily Indebted Poor Countries (HIPC) Debt Initiative (Torres 8).

It is clear that beneath the few main official languages, associated with their respective colonial pasts, the Americas live in a highly complex linguistic reality, often hidden in regional diagnoses and studies; however, this plurilingual reality is not properly acknowledged in education policies and programs. The Caribbean, for example, demonstrates institutionalized approaches to subtracting plurilingualism. In the majority of the English- and French-speaking countries in the Caribbean, the first language of the population is a Creole. In Guyana, Jamaica, and Haiti,

Creole is related to the official language, French. In Dominica and St. Lucia, English is the official language, but the main spoken language is Kwéyòl, a French-based Creole. In Suriname, where the official language is Dutch, what is spoken in everyday practice is Sranan Tongo, an English-based Creole (Torres 14–15).

Nevertheless, in all these countries, except for Haiti, education—including literacy classes for adults—is conducted in the official language. Those who attend school speaking a minoritized language become adept at shuttling across languages as they negotiate the different and home language by self-censorship during their schooling. Still, a monolingual orientation is dominant in all nations of the Americas; because of this, I believe that more discussions must happen across fields, principally among educators who define literacy for various nations. Local bilinguals recognize the power differential between languages. The United Nations has both helped and hindered movements that recognize the dignity of local languages and literacies across nations. Since its founding in 1945, the United Nations's Educational, Scientific and Cultural Organization (UNESCO) has:

> [P]lanned and implemented a vast number of developmental and cooperative projects concerning education in the wide sense; but cultural creativity, cultural rights and ethnic/racial discrimination have also been important concerns to the UNESCO since the beginning.... A large number of writings supported or published by the UNESCO have over the past five decades made important contributions to international debates about racism, ethnocentrism, cultural relativism, cultural hegemonies, education, and quests for equal cultural rights. (Erickson 128)

It is UNESCO's work with literacy in the Americas, however, that this section examines next.

UNESCO's definition of literacy is "the ability to use printed and written information to function in society, to achieve one's goals, and to develop one's knowledge and potential" ("Education"). It is telling that literacy, by this definition, is both individualized (i.e., "achieve one's goals") and related to "development"—two hemispheric ideals that "trickle down" from the north, along with the conditions attached to those World Bank loans that falsely promote development in name but austerity in practice. I want to step away from this developmental definition, but note that the UNESCO definition establishes a base for nations of the Americas that intend to meet standards established elsewhere, while drawing up their own definitions. The following are a few definitions from around the Americas drawn from the 2009 UNESCO regional synthesis report, "From Literacy to Lifelong Learning: Trends, Issues and Challenges in Youth and Adult Education in Latin America and the Caribbean," by Rosa María Torres. They are notions of adult literacy in three nations. I have emphasized certain words and phrases in boldface:

> *Guatemala*: "Literacy is understood as the initial systematic stage of integral basic education. It also implies the **development of skills and knowledge that respond to the socio-cultural and economic productive needs of the population**. This initial phase consists in learning to read, write and **calculate basic mathematical problems**: post-literacy is the follow-up, reinforcement and expansion stage towards integral basic education that is motivational and practical, in the sense of providing immediate benefits to the newly-literate person."
>
> *Haiti*: "Making a person literate in Haiti is leaving him/her apt for reading and writing in a **fluid manner**, and in Creole, a small text of about **15 lines**, and also **to maintain and even develop this skill throughout his/her life**."
>
> *Suriname*: "A person is literate when he/she is able to read and write and **especially in Dutch**" (Torres 15)

All three countries' definitions address communicative practices, including—as for Guatemala—numeracy. Yet at the same time, they reinforce a monolingualized orientation toward hegemonic literacies in their differing contexts. The last definition from Suriname is telling: "a person is literate when he/she is able to read and write *especially* in Dutch"—the dominant language, a legacy of European colonialism. All the definitions turn literacy toward the individual, to a personal responsibility to develop "post-literacy" as in the Guatemalan example, or for reading 15 lines of Creole in Haiti. The undertones of neoliberal claims for level, meritocratic playing fields and racialized and ethnicized inequalities inherent to the rule of the free market in the above definitions most assuredly steer me in formulating a rigorous theoretical political economic grounding. In addition, methodological knowledge—again, constantly revised and enriched by cross-field collaborations—will deepen with a translingual framework in conversation with hemispheric studies that accounts for plurilingual contexts.

In plurilingual settings, decisions to make use of one language or another depend on the perceived prestige, status, or desirability of one language over another. The social statuses of all languages are closely related to economic status (Bourdieu; Canagarajah; Lippi-Green); however, in the case of the Americas, the logic of coloniality privileges European languages. Where a minority language coexists with poverty, social deprivation, and unemployment, the social status of the language is affected. When a majority language is seen as giving higher social status and political power, a shift toward majority language use may occur. For example, Castilian Spanish—a fictional, European standard version of that language—equates for some with material wealth and security as forms of good living and economic upward mobility. The order of linguistic distinction and symbolic power hierarchically arranged produces linguistic distinctions. Such differences mark transnational conceptions of assimilation, social mobility, identity, and resistance from Canada to Chile.

In the final section of this chapter, I further explore a composition course that seeks to delink from monolingualized assumptions about literacy in the context of the United States, specifically the plurilingual state of California. From the delinking lens applied to local literacies, a translingual approach accounts for how the expansion and contraction of a unified global market dictate geopolitics, and how languages that cross borders are policed.

LANGUAGE HYBRIDITY IN THE AMERICAS AND DELINKING MONOLINGUAL ORIENTATIONS TO LITERACY

In composition courses that embrace a translingual orientation to literacy, structured goals should include assessments of institutional definitions of literacy across contexts and local practices of literacy amid social struggles about language standardization in the Americas. Students' composition or writing projects should engage with critical discourses through formal and informal avenues, openly embracing a translingual orientation for minoritized language and literacy practices. I argue for composition pedagogies that frame, conceptualize, interpret, and highlight the plurality of local histories and social struggles informing translocal emergent multiethnic, translingual, and transnational of the present and the future. Composition pedagogy grounded in social justice and democratic pluralism must connect challenges to inequalities; however, with Composition, the focus on writing and using language must also be used both to build critiques and to compose expressive projects that reflect translocal struggles and histories.

A focus on the translocal means incorporating literacy research into the practices of communities, following the movements in diverse activities, performances, and genres, including across languages, generations, and social classes (Lorimer Leonard). Educators who recognize the translingual repertoires of students acknowledge an additive approach to language learning (Canagarajah; García; Horner, Lu, Royster, and Trimbur). The translingual view may remain contrary to language purists, but the translingual orientation also acknowledges the hybridity of everyday practices plurilingual communities develop in the contexts in which they are situated. In the Americas, for example, *Spanglish* embodies plurilingual contact and hybridity.

Rather than conceiving of Spanglish as illegitimate or nonstandard English and/or Spanish, a translingual approach to linguistic hybridity celebrates what Ilan Stavans describes as the dance of rhythm and thought *entre la flexibilidad y el dogmatismo* of standardization in the fusion of *inglés* and Spanish across the Americas. Transnational Spanglish and its rumba with standardized literacies are not only legitimate expressions for dominant cultural discourses for communication, but also the struggle for legitimacy, despite local popularity, is a hallmark of critical moves delinking from hegemonic literacies. With this in mind, a translingual orientation to Composition examines Spanglish in conversation with standardized English in cultural practices so as to question current arguments for (and in) its deployment as a translanguaging repertoire and legitimate literacy practice rather than simply a response to standardization. The translingual *retórica* of Spanglish converses the creative dance of hybridized languaging with the criticality of *conocimiento*, of knowledge of the rhetorical situation and audience awareness.

The translingual *retórica* of Spanglish on one level is a practical debunking of the theoretical elaboration of *mestizaje* in the Americas. Historically, mestizaje and miscegenation organized castes according to race, which produced social inequalties related to linguistic attributes tied to race. The castes of distinction remain in the postcolonial version—that is, they are masked by hegemonic categories that ignore demographic mixtures, translating them into linguistic distinctions and symbolic power. Likewise, they intersect in relation to Latinx and Latin American hybridized uses of Spanglish to articulate conceptions of assimilation, social mobility, identity, and resistance.

Mestizaje, however, can also be a tool for delinking marginalized discourses surrounding local logics from dominant discourses of standardization. For example, critical readings from various disciplines complement the transformational potential of the Spanglish approach to Translingual

Literacy Studies, shuttling between performance studies, sociolinguistics, linguistic anthropology, sociology of education and immigration, and bilingual pedagogy. However, focusing on aspects of social justice and language standardization has the most potential to uncover motivations for delinking from hegemonic literacies.

In the United States, the hegemony of English is well documented. In 1998, for example, California voters passed Proposition 227, mandating that the state eliminate bilingual education programs. As a result, thousands of emergent bilingual students were marked as "limited"—in their English monolingualism—and therefore were moved from bilingual programs into mainstream English classrooms. For Composition students not in this predicament, imagining the collision of contact zones in such an unwelcoming climate to bilingual education seems, frankly, foreign. For monolingual students, it is pivotal to probe their languages and identities as members of communities that are mythologized as monolingual in name only. Likewise, students who do not identify as multilingual also should learn to empathize with an additive translingual orientation to literacy.

Proposition 227 offers not only a window into the legacy of internal colonialism in the United States, but also into the resiliency of communities who grapple with structures imposed on their home languages. The 2009 short film *Immersion*, directed by Richard Levien, narrates the predicament of a recently migrated, creative emergent bilingual student coping with his home language being taken away in elementary school as a result of the California law. *Immersion* dramatizes the day-to-day practices of multilingual students negotiating monolingualized cultural assumptions about standardization, and it has appeal to both audiences in multiple languages. As the film demonstrates, the translingual view acknowledges the hybridity of everyday practices emergent bilingual individuals and communities develop in diverse contexts, and students and adults in the film fluidly use Spanglish in private or secretly.

For students, writing about the film offers a window into how literacy practices align and conflict in ways that both correlate and contrast with the literacies promoted by legislation and institutionalized in schools, as well as local strategies to nurture the dignity of translingual literacy repertoires (Canagarajah; Horner et al.). A translingual connection to various groups crosses languages and also comes into conflicts of power though leveling the inequalities inherent in monolingual assumptions about standardization.

Immersion also opens a space for exploration of immigration as a topic of research and argument invention. Immigration, as part of national and transnational migration broadly conceived, concerns a drastic change in social environments and has profound transformative and symbolic effects for individuals, families, and for generations of potential social futures. Migration, emigration, and immigration transform cultures and, in theory, transform the processes of individual and group deculturation, acculturation, and transculturation when navigating the social order(s) of the sending and receiving nations and/or regions.

In the United States, immigration entails extensive state policing, or the governmental arm of legitimate force, control, and discipline that enforces citizenship and securing borders. Severe state disciplining and discrimination and strong reactionary ethnic identification circularly affect one another; generationally, how one incorporates ethnic identity takes a variety of forms, ranging from homogenization as an "American," to a variety of ethnic "hyphenated" Americans, or "minorities." Ultimately, schools bear the responsibility for producing conscientious citizens, so the intolerant impetus behind Proposition 227 and efforts to standardize students and their languages do not follow the democratic tradition of schooling.

These types of intolerant linguistic policies are directly challenged by Mignolo is delinking when applied to pedagogy.

The delinking method is one for un-learning in order to learn, of reorienting to self-reflexivity, of interrogating ideological intersections and institutional constraints leading to misperceived categories that privilege hegemonic literacies or, rather, various disciplinary literacies that make their own power legitimate.

Delinking entails the ability to *re-read* the world and the opportunity to *re-write* it. This is where Rhetoric and Composition offers the liberating potential to envision social justice across languages. Finally, this chapter nods to a translingual orientation to literacy practices and translanguaging repertoires of students, extending the asset-based pedagogies' research that honors, explores, and extends the strengths of communities. It advocates for literacy researchers to join conversations with scholars whose works lead Rhetoric and Composition and Literacy Studies farther in "trans" (i.e., -lingual, -languaging, -national, -literacies, -generational, -cultural) analytic frameworks across disciplines. Translingual literacy research into the language and literacy practices of emergent bilinguals and bilingual communities would work from a method of delinking of standardized notions of official literacies to challenge the reproduction of social inequalities.

WORKS CITED

Anthias, Floya. Hierarchies of Social Location, Class and Intersectionality: Towards a Translocational Frame. *International Sociology* 28 (2012): 121–138. Print.

Baca, Damián. *Mestiz@ Scripts, Digital Migrations, and the Territories of Writing.* New York: Palgrave, 2008. Print.

Baca, Damián, and Victor Villanueva, eds. *Rhetorics of the Americas: 3114 BCE to 2012 CE.* New York: Palgrave, 2010. Print.

Bourdieu, Pierre. *Distinction: A Social Critique of the Judgment of Taste.* Trans. Richard Nice. Cambridge: Harvard UP, 1984. Print.

Canagarajah, A. Suresh. *Translingual Practice: Global Englishes and Cosmopolitan Relations.* New York: Routledge, 2013. Print.

Education: Literacy. *United Nations Educational, Scientific and Cultural Organization.* United Nations, n.d. Web. March 31, 2015.

Eriksen, Thomas Hylland. Between Universalism and Relativism: A Critique of the UNESCO Concept of Culture. In *Culture and Rights: Anthropological Perspectives*, eds. Jane K. Cowan, Marie-Bénédicte Dembour, and Richard A. Wilson, 127–148. New York: Cambridge UP, 2001.

García, Ofelia. *Bilingual Education in the 21st Century: A Global Perspective.* New York: Wiley and Blackwell, 2011. Print.

Hernandez-Zamora, Gregorio. *Decolonizing Literacy: Mexican Lives in the Era of Global Capitalism.* Bristol, UK: Multilingual Matters, 2010. Print.

Horner, Bruce, and Min-Zhan Lu. Resisting Monolingualism in 'English': Reading and Writing the Politics of Language. In *Rethinking English in Schools: A New and Constructive Stage*, eds. Viv Ellis, Carol Fox, and Brian Street, 141–157. London: Continuum, 2007. Print.

Horner, Bruce, Min-Zhan Lu, Jacqueline Jones Royster, and John Trimbur. Language Difference in Writing: Toward a Translingual Approach. *College English* 73, no. 3 (2011): 299–317. Print.

Immersion. Dir. Richard Levien. Perf. Gerardo Acevedo, Nabor Acevedo, and Antonio Acosta. Widdershins, 2009. Film.

Kalman, Judy, and Brian Street, eds. *Literacy and Numeracy in Latin America: Local Perspectives and Beyond.* New York: Routledge, 2013. Print.

Lippi-Green, Rosina. *English With an Accent: Language, Ideology, and Discrimination in the United States.* New York: Routledge, 1997. Print.

Lorimer Leonard, Rebecca. Traveling Literacies: Multilingual Writing on the Move. *Research in the Teaching of English* 48, no. 1 (2013): 13–39. Print.

Mignolo, Walter D. Delinking: The Rhetoric of Modernity, the Logic of Coloniality, and the Grammar of De-Coloniality. *Cultural Studies* 21, no. 2–3 (2007): 449–514. Print.

Stavans, Ilan. *Spanglish: The Making of a New American Language.* New York: HarperCollins, 2003. Print.

Torres, Rosa María. From Literacy to Lifelong Learning: Trends, Issues and Challenges in Youth and Adult Education in Latin America and the Caribbean: Regional Synthesis Report. *From Literacy to Lifelong Learning: Towards the Challenges of the XXI Century, Mexico City, 10–13 Sept. 2008.* Hamburg: UNESCO Institute for Lifelong Learning, n.d. 2009. Web. March 31, 2015.

CHAPTER 3

Citizenship

Ana Milena Ribero

On August 30, 2013, 34 undocumented migrants wearing graduation caps and gowns stood in line at the US Port of Entry at Laredo, Texas, and waited to enter the United States. These young migrants, popularly known as DREAMers due to their support of the DREAM Act,[1] had lived a large portion of their lives in the United States and had been deported or had "self-deported" to the countries of their births. They now stood at the door of the US and asked to return to the country they considered their home.

The *Dream 30*, as these demonstrators have been called, are part of the *Bring Them Home* campaign organized by the National Immigrant Youth Alliance (NIYA), a network of grassroots organizations led by undocumented youth who believe that the migrant rights fight in the United States is to be fought on the streets as well as in the halls of government. Committed to "achieving equality for all immigrant youth, regardless of their legal status" (National Immigrant Youth Alliance), NIYA advocates for a grassroots effort based on civil disobedience that positions undocumented youth at the forefront of the migrant rights movement. Their most famous operation to date has been the *Bring Them Home Campaign*,

A.M. Ribero (✉)
School of Writing, Literature, and Film, Oregon State University, Corvallis, OR, USA

which, according to NIYA activist Mohammad Abdollahi, aims to highlight the family separation resulting from US immigration policies, including the skyrocketing number of deportations under the Obama administration and state policies that encourage "self-deportation" such as Alabama's House Bill 56 and Arizona's State Bill 1070 (Nevarez).

Events such as the *Dream 30* demonstration highlight the complexity of national belonging in the contemporary moment. Although citizenship has traditionally been approached as a juridical position dependent on birthright or naturalization, this construct does not account for people like the *Dream 30* activists, people who—despite having been board abroad—have lived here most of their lives, consider this country their home, and feel national allegiance to the United States. While DREAMers may consider themselves American culturally, traditional legal definitions of citizenship refuse to recognize them. The DREAMers' exclusion from US citizenry and the refusal of the US government—and largely, as well, of the US population—to imagine a US citizenship that may include these migrant Others highlights that, regardless of more humane and dynamic theorizations of national belonging (Flores and Benmayor 1998), citizenship in its essence is built on exclusions that are largely based on racialized, gendered, and sexualized identities.[2]

Although the definition of *citizenship* is flexible and can be construed as much more than a juridical status, I argue that citizenship is always already exclusionary and therefore cannot truly be decolonized. Instead, as Chandra Talpade Mohanty argues, "the challenge, then, is to find ways of conceptualizing community differently without dismissing its appeal and importance" (85). Recognizing the inescapable contradictions that our desire for belonging entails, our decolonial imaginings must envision an alternative to citizenship as a rights-bearing state of being.

In the pages that follow, I outline how citizenship is always already constituted through colonialist discourses of belonging that not only exclude minoritized Others locally but also serve the global dominance of Western nation-states. My analysis of citizenship does not intend to be fatalistic or overly idealistic; instead, I launch a decolonial critique of this current conceptualization of belonging to emphasize that, for people of color, inclusion in citizenship and other dominant forms of belonging requires a reiterative practice of legitimization as they push to be recognized in a framework that depends on their exclusion.

My analysis explores how citizenship as a racialized rights-bearing status forwards the unequal distribution of benefits that not only affects the well-being of citizens and (non)citizens living within a particular geopolitical boundary but also enables the current world order and its neocolonialist practices. Citizenship reifies the coloniality of power, as Walter Mignolo suggests, to subalternize racialized knowledges (12). Decolonial critique, therefore, must analyze citizenship through the lens of the racialized coloniality of power to explore how it maintains Euroamerican hegemony globally and white heteropatriarchy locally.

As the building block of the nation-state—itself a requisite for the workings of neocolonialism and neoliberalism—citizenship helps to delineate and reinforce national borders that constitute global hierarchies of social, political, military, and economic power, hierarchies that disproportionately benefit the Global North at the expense of the racialized peoples of the Global South. In tracing the racialized and racializing characteristics of citizenship, I hope to make visible the inescapable exclusionary underpinnings of this construct. Citizenship is constituted via exclusion and therefore cannot be reclaimed inasmuch as decoloniality holds equality as its objective.

In the United States, citizenship as stipulated by the Fourteenth Amendment's principle of *jus soli* has been racialized from its inception. Because it was designed to address the citizenship of the children of former slaves, the broad statement about citizenship in the Amendment that "all persons born or naturalized in the United States, and subject to the jurisdiction thereof, are citizens of the United States and of the State wherein they reside" had racializing implications for US citizenship. Whereas the Fourteenth Amendment outlined the right to citizenship for the black children of former slaves, whites never needed a law to legitimize their claims to *jus soli* birthright citizenship.

The principle of *jus soli* raised questions about who could be considered a US citizen, specifically as the US-born children of racialized (non)citizen Others began claiming citizenship under the Amendment. In 1898, the Supreme Court ruled on the case of the United States *vs.* Wong Kim Ark that US-born children of foreign nationals would qualify for US citizenship under the Fourteenth Amendment (Schmid 49). Sociologist Carol Schmid explains that despite this Supreme Court decision, challenges to the principle of *jus soli* have increased during the last decade as a result of heightened public awareness of undocumented migration into the country and intensified discourses of post-9/11 jingoism (49).

Current challenges to birthright citizenship, such as the Birthright Citizenship Act introduced by the House of Representatives in 2009, have sought to deny *jus soli* to the children of undocumented US residents. Relying on the rhetorical figure of the "anchor baby," nationalist challenges to birthright citizenship illustrate how bodies of color are marked as threatening and (non)belonging within traditional discourses of citizenship. According to anthropologist Leo Chávez, the anchor baby metaphor refers to the alleged practice of undocumented Latinx families giving birth on US soil so that their children can be granted US citizenship through *jus soli*, thus enabling the families to petition for legal residence through laws that privilege family reunification (88).

Through *jus soli* citizenship, the undocumented migrant, who is always already Latinx in the national imaginary, becomes a threat to the racially homogeneous nation. Sociologists Carmen Lugo-Lugo and Mary Bloodsworth-Lugo insist that in post-9/11 rhetoric, the anchor baby and the less popular "terror baby" have become salient rhetorical figures that posit migrant women of color as threats to the safety of the nation-state and its white, neoliberal citizenry. Although anchor babies supposedly threaten the United States by forwarding the Latinization of the nation—the browning of America—terror babies, believed to be US born from women sent to the country by terrorist organizations, purportedly pose a violent threat to the nation because of their terrorist connections and the ease of cross-border migration made possible by their *jus soli* US citizenship.

Politicians and pundits use the rhetorical figures of anchor and terror babies to posit that "immigrant women are weaponizing reproduction, such that their babies become the equivalent of bombs being 'dropped' in hospitals to be deployed at a later time against the American public" (Lugo-Lugo and Bloodsworth-Lugo 16). Through these two prevalent rhetorical figures in dominant discourses of migration, bodies of color become newly dangerous because they not only supposedly threaten the safety of the nation but also portend demographic changes to the racial make-up of US citizenry. Bodies of color are feared from birth, constituted as the deviant and dangerous Other to the normative citizen. Citizenship thus is constituted as white; citizens of color, even when sanctioned through birthright, pose a threat to the nation's stability.

In addition to the racialized characteristics of the principle of *jus soli*, US citizenship excludes racialized Others through US naturalization law. As Queer and Gender Studies scholar Siobhan Somerville outlines, there is an explicit exclusion of racialized Others in the very inception of US citizenship. Referring specifically to the Naturalization Act of 1790, Somerville writes: "This law clearly and quite self-consciously restricted naturalization to 'free white persons,' thus racializing naturalized American citizenship at the very moment in which it was codified as a legal status. In fact, the [Naturalization Act of 1790] was the first federally enacted law that referred to race explicitly" (667).

In addition to excluding people of color and other migrants not considered white, the Naturalization Act assumed that US citizenship would be gendered and sexualized in heteropatriarchal ways: "this earliest juridical statement on naturalization presumed that the prospective citizen would be not only white and free but also a (potential) parent" (Somerville 667). Thus, the borders of citizenship drawn at the very birth of the United States as a nation-state excluded racialized, gendered, and sexualized subjects to reinforce notions of a white heteronormative and patriarchal civic imaginary through naturalization laws.

Passage of migrant-phobic legislation, including Arizona's "Support Our Law Enforcement and Safe Neighborhoods Act," also known as SB 1070, illustrates how citizenship continues to be patrolled along racialized lines. Passed in 2010, SB 1070 requires US (non)citizens to carry documentation proving their legal presence and makes violating this requirement a state misdemeanor—before SB 1070, such a violation was considered a federal misdemeanor only. It thus forces state law enforcement agencies to act as immigration officials and enforce federal immigration laws (State of Arizona). Communications scholar Josue David Cisneros explores how SB 1070 not only forces people of color to constantly rationalize their citizenship but also places responsibility on police officers to become "critics of behaviors and demeanors, judging who performed citizenship ... and whose performance communicated an affect of 'alienness'" (112). SB 1070 creates a framework for the performance of citizenship and the policing of those performances with clear racialized characteristics.

Because SB 1070 was enacted in the geopolitical location of the US–Mexico border and within a discursive economy that sees the undocumented migrant as always already Mexican, the law marks the affect of (non)belonging as decidedly and stereotypically Mexican. Citizenship, then, is marked on the body through phenotypical characteristics (e.g., skin color, hair texture) and social traits (e.g., clothing, mannerisms, language use). It is interesting to note that the racialized aspect of the performance of citizenship implies that not only must the undocumented and the migrant perform citizenship correctly but also that *all* brown bodies must do so. (Non)belonging is conflated with *Mexicanidad*, which is itself conflated with *Latinidad*. Thus, all Latinx brown bodies are suspect. However, the racialization of citizenship also is nuanced.

Light-skinned Latinxs or those of higher socioeconomic status may be able to perform citizenship correctly and therefore are not so highly policed, while darker-skinned Latinxs and other people of color find their belonging repeatedly questioned. As Cisneros writes, "the undocumented immigrant [and, I add, other people of color] [have] become responsible for [their] own alienization not only because of [their assumed] 'illegal act' of border crossing but also because [they fail] to adequately give the impression that [they] belong" (118). SB 1070 made it so that the actual border crossing does not terminally mark the undocumented as (non) belonging; it is the inability to perform citizenship correctly, as defined by racialized characteristics, that ultimately marginalizes people of color from the US civic imaginary.

It follows then that citizenship and the (non)citizen are caught in a complex co-constitutive relationship, a relationship replete with race, gender, sex, and class implications that aim at maintaining a homogeneous ahistorical idea of US citizenry. Because citizenship is defined by inclusion (and exclusion), the excluded Other shapes the boundaries of inclusion. And in our contemporary moment, as it has been throughout US history, the excluded Other is a racialized, gendered, and sexualized subject—the young black male, the woman of color, the queer and/or transgender person, the brown undocumented migrant, and so on. I focus my analysis of citizenship on this latter figure—the undocumented Latinx migrant—because this figure has become the rhetorical apex of (non)citizen discourses.

Examples abound in popular media reflecting how the racialized characteristics of citizenship are (re)inscribed around the rhetorical figure of the undocumented Latinx. For example, on September 14, 2014, the satirical news program, *The Daily Show*, featured a segment titled "No Country for Little Kids" in which correspondent Michael Che illustrated the disproportionate and often absurd fear-mongering that occurs when the borders of the nation are militarized against the undocumented Latinx migrant. In a satirical interview of Jim Gilchrist, founder of the vigilante militia group The Minuteman Project, Che reported on "Operation Normandy," group's response to the increasing number of unaccompanied minors crossing the US–Mexico border without proper documentation.[3]

"Operation Normandy"—the title an allusion that Gilchrist hoped would connote the immensity and intensity of the protest (but that, as Che noted, likened the USA to the Nazis fighting against the Allied Forces in World War II)—capitalizes on public fears that unaccompanied minors are, as Gilchrist told Che, "a vanguard of a larger invasion which will lead to the demise of our nation as a global economic power." Gilchrist is not alone in his fear. During the summer of 2014, which was the peak of public paranoia about Central American undocumented, unaccompanied minors, references to children as "invaders" were popular in US legislative discourse, news outlets, and social media.[4]

"Operation Normandy" illustrates how a discursive emphasis on the dangers of undocumented migration leads to popular panics regarding the effects of racialized Others on a citizenship that is always already imagined as white and heteropatriarchal. Operation Normandy is about more than stopping child migrants at the border; it is about policing the liminal boundaries of a national imaginary that desires racial homogeneity. For Gilchrist, The Minuteman Project volunteers protect the nation from what he terms "the Latinization of America," which would bring about a bilingual nation where Latinxs exert influence in the daily running of society. Through discourses and practices that aim to position racialized undocumented migrants as the binary Other to the white heteronormative citizen, the decision of who gets to claim normative belonging and the right to the pursuit of happiness that *that* belonging allegedly entails is made along racialized lines that aim to create a supposedly homogenous US citizenry. Citizenship as currently construed cannot escape the discriminatory discourses that constitute it.

The discursive and legislative criminalization that frames undocumented migrants and other people of color as threats to the nation-state also underscores the dialectic relationship between those who will always already be excluded from US citizenry and those who normatively fit within it. There is no nation, and therefore there is no citizen, without the (non)citizen body to define in opposition. And, as the embodiment of (non)belonging, the undocumented migrant occupies the position opposite the citizen in the national consciousness. This citizen–(non)citizen binary is largely (re)produced by immigration policies that result in the category of "illegal alien"—an underclass of excluded subjects who are denied the opportunity to adjust their legal status. This perpetual illegality ensures a cheap labor force for capital and convenes an Orwellian common enemy against whom to unite the nation.

Contrary to popular belief, the growing number of undocumented migrants in the United States does not solely reflect an increase in migrants who are supposedly "skipping the line" of legal entry and crossing the border with no regard for the rule of law. Instead, the growing undocumented population indicates the effect of legislation that increased the size of the category of "illegal." Immigration legislation works as a discourse of colonial power through a rhetorical framework that defines normative entry and legal citizenship, and normalizes dominant narratives about immigration that absolve legislators from their role in contributing to the undocumented population. For example, even though President Obama tried to soften his stance on immigration by claiming that his administration would focus on apprehending and deporting "criminal aliens" and deeming those without criminal histories a "low priority" for deportation, any migrant who has been deported is defined as a "criminal alien" thanks to immigration legislation passed during the George W. Bush administration.

As sociologist Heidy Sarabia states, "[a]s a 'criminal alien' with a past conviction, undocumented presence in the United States is enough to serve jail time" (57), as well as to be denied the possibility of ever legalizing one's residency status. Although Obama's claim of prioritizing the deportation of "criminal aliens" over that of families seems to target undocumented migrants who may have committed gang violence, theft, or drug-related crimes (themselves gendered and racialized constructs in the national consciousness), in actuality Obama's policy prioritizes the detention and deportation of migrants who have reentered the country after deportation. These illegalized migrants who may have no criminal record other than their deportation join the population of the perpetually illegal because their criminalization denies them the ability to ever adjust their legal status.

Sarabia posits that rather than deterring unauthorized immigration, such immigration policies serve various purposes for the state: "On the one hand, [immigration legislation] helps to discipline one segment of the labor force (by making 'illegal' workers vulnerable). On the other hand, illegality creates monolithic notions of national identity (by delineating who legitimately belongs and who does not)" (61). Serving the coloniality of power, immigration legislation guards the borders of citizenship by stipulating and policing the boundaries of illegality and working as neoliberal disciplinary systems for labor subordination through nationalist means.

But immigration legislation, as queer studies scholar Eithne Luibheid reminds us, "[functions] in a double sense: as the means to delimit the nation, citizenry and citizenship *and, conversely, as the loci for contesting and reworking these limits*" (xi, emphasis added). Citizenship as a discursive construct is not monolithic. Its meaning is subject to power and power's corollary: resistance. A decolonial critique of citizenship not only recognizes it as inherently exclusionary but also acknowledges that, for people of color, citizenship is an oppositional practice that reflects the desire for recognition and the rights that supposedly come with it. Demonstrations such as the *Dream 30* events highlight how the (non)citizen's desire for the nation-state results in iterations of belonging that (re)constitute citizenship in ways not yet sanctioned by dominant discourses. As Judith Butler and Gayatri Chakravorty Spivak suggest:

> The call for that exercise of freedom that comes with citizenship ... starts to take what it asks for. ... [T]o make the demand on freedom is already to begin its exercise and then to ask for its legitimation is to also announce the gap between its exercise and its realization and to put both into public discourse in a way so that that gap is seen, so that that gap can mobilize. (68)

The gap between the exercise and realization of citizenship that Butler and Spivak allude to is key to my decolonial critique of citizenship. It is this gap that positions citizenship always on the horizon yet forever out of reach for racialized Others in the United States.

Resistance to dominant citizenship discourses, such as the demonstrations in the *Bring Them Home* campaign, can be read not only as new enunciations of citizenship that challenge racial homogeneity but also as racialized formations that expose the paradox of citizenship as a rights-bearing form of belonging, where even performances of citizenship that align with traditional conceptualizations of the construct (i.e., neoliberal principles of the modern nation-state) are "still not quite" satisfactory when they come from racialized Others. This is the paradox highlighted in citizenship performances by (non)sanctioned, (non)citizen Others such as the DREAMers: as the rights-bearing status of the rights-deserving citizen subject, citizenship is always already exclusionary, can never be embodied by the racialized Other, therefore cannot forward sincere decolonial designs.

Because dominant ideas of national(ist) belonging are predicated on who is recognized as a citizen subject, the national imaginary largely depends on the subject's ability to perform citizenship successfully according to certain discursive standards, and on whether those performances are intelligible within dominant discourses of citizenship. Consequently, as Mohanty suggests, the nation-state is "inherently unstable, contextual ... and it is the product of interpretation, interpretation based on an attention to history, to the concrete, to what Foucault has called subjugated knowledges" (104). It is significant to note, however, that the practices of embodied citizenship of people of color are often not received as demonstrations of citizenship because bodies of color are always already understood as too divergent from normatively constituted citizen bodies. Consequently, bodies of color may always remain outside dominant discourses of citizenship, regardless of how well they can perform it.

For example, much as been said about how protests by people of color are perceived in light of the 2014 demonstrations responding to the shooting of black unarmed teenager Michael Brown and the Grand Jury decision not to indict his killer, Ferguson Police Department Officer Darren Wilson. The militarized practices of the police against black demonstrators illustrate how performances of citizenship by people of color are unintelligible as anything other than deviant in the popular imaginary. In an opinion piece in *The Washington Post*, African American Studies scholar Carol Anderson argues that while acts of rage by people of color are portrayed in the media as "savage" and "mob-like," acts of white rage are governmentally sanctioned and portrayed as reasonable and "civil." The civility of the normative white citizen is juxtaposed against the savagery of the person of color, echoing the racist colonial discourses used to rationalize the theft of native land and the enslavement of African peoples, and pushing black Americans to the edge of civic imaginary.

Activist and author Sally Kohn illustrates this disparity of representation when she compares media portrayals of the Ferguson protests with those of the Pumpkin Festival riots in Keene, New Hampshire. Kohn writes:

> The protesters in Ferguson were airing legitimate grievances through mostly peaceful means and yet were denigrated [by the media], while the [white] rioters in Keene were merely part of a party that "spun out of control"— Never mind that those in Keene were reportedly drunk and dangerous and disproportionately violent.

As Anderson and Kohn posit, while unruly bodies of color are quickly ascribed the labels of "savage" and "mob" and used to rationalize the marginalization of entire minoritized communities, white bodies are seldom generalized in such ways and their behavior is often explained as an example of "boys being boys." The "unruly" behaviors of people of color are juxtaposed to the "civil" or at least reasonable behavior of whites to reify the racialized line between citizen and (non)citizen.

This critical look at the racialized portrayal of protest highlights the fact that although blacks may have rights to US citizenship, their bodies are read as Other—as de facto (non)citizens—making their performances unintelligible within dominant discourses of citizenship. The gap between the exercise of citizenship and its realization keeps black people at the margins of the US civic imaginary despite their de jure claims to citizenship and its rights.

Similarly, laws that encourage racial profiling, such as SB 1070 in Arizona or the "Stand Your Ground" law in Florida, are both causes and effects of the perpetual exclusion of bodies of color from US citizenship. Such laws and the practices they engender highlight the performativity of citizenship. Citizenship becomes an outwardly legible characteristic, effected through performance by an "actor" and through reception by an "audience." In other words, if belonging is evidenced on one's body, then it is evoked and understood through its repeated performance. And within exclusionary discourses of citizenship, bodies of color are always marked as (non)belonging. Regardless of their juridical citizenship status, bodies of color are often not understood as normative citizens within the national imaginary and their performances of citizenship are not read as such by their audience.

When bodies of color are unintelligible as anything other than Other, the exclusionary borders of citizenship are (re)drawn to support the hegemony of whiteness both locally and globally. As historical sociologist Margaret Somers reminds us in her influential work on citizenship in neoliberal contexts: "A benign view of citizenship has purchase only from the perspective of the insiders. [Citizenship] is the cold instrument of exclusion to those outside its borders, both internal borders based on race and gender exclusion, as well as nation-state ones based on xenophobia and nationalism" (5). Citizenship, with its exclusionary underpinnings, serves to buttress nationalist discourses of fear and jingoism that constitute the nation-state—the organizing structure of colonial/modern power. The racialized dimensions of US citizenship, themselves created discursively and performatively as effects of colonial power, neoliberal ideology, and a pervasively xenophobic national imaginary, directly contribute to neocolonial regimes of power that depend on a racialized and dehumanized labor force for the production of capital and the reproduction of racist hegemonies. The person of color and the undocumented migrant, as racialized and dehumanized bodies, are vehicles for the reproduction of this power.

DREAMers, who are always already racialized, have become the focus of national anxiety about the changing demographics of the US citizenry, so much so that the DREAM Act has sat in Congress for more than a decade without being passed despite enjoying occasional bipartisan support. The recurring failure of the DREAM Act illustrates how the racialization, demonization, and criminalization of young US Latinx migrants contributes to their exclusion from the civic imaginary. Citizenship, as the apex of neoliberal power, reifies the coloniality of power that (re)produces and depends on the exclusion of racialized Others. This is why citizenship cannot be reappropriated with egalitarian consequences. DREAMer rights movements illustrate how claims to rights based on citizenship or on national belonging are made at the expense of others.

When the *Dream 30* argue that they belong in the United States, they define the terms of that belonging in ways that inevitably exclude other oppressed groups. Mohanty reminds us of the "irreconcilable tension between the search for a secure place from which to speak, within which to act, and the awareness of the price at which secure places are bought, the awareness of the exclusions, the denials, the blindnesses on which they are predicated" (101). The cost of our investment in citizenship as a secure place from which to speak and to act is always the exclusion of those Others who will never be considered citizens.

Perhaps rather than reappropriate this weighty term, we should imagine a truly decolonial future in which citizenship is unveiled for the chimera that it is. This will require us to embrace what Mohanty calls "not being home," and to realize "that home was an illusion of coherence and safety based on the exclusion of specific histories of oppression and resistance, the repression of differences even within oneself" (90). As I have tried to show, citizenship produces and is produced by the illusion of homogeneity, a pretense that as decolonial scholars we can no longer accept.

NOTES

1. The DREAM Act (Development, Relief, and Education for Alien Minors) was introduced in the US Senate in August 2001 as a way to provide legal relief for undocumented young people who were brought into the United States by their parents as children. Although the DREAM Act has changed since its initial drafting, the primary elements include a pathway toward legalization for undocumented immigrants who entered the country before the age of 16, have been here for five years or more, have "good moral character," graduated from a US high school or received a GED, and have been accepted to a four-year university or completed two years of US military service. (United States)

2. Although in this text I only delve into the racialized dimensions of citizenship, I recommend Lugones (2007) for a feminist critique of how the coloniality of power also is gendered and sexualized.

3. *The New York Times* reported that 68,000 unaccompanied minors were apprehended crossing the border in 2014, doubling the previous year's numbers. President Obama called this an "urgent humanitarian situation" and on July 8, 2014, asked Congress for $3.7 billion to ameliorate various aspects of this issue. The so-called crisis had its peak of media and public attention in the summer of 2014 and has more recently all but vanished from the public sphere. (Park)

4. During a speech on the floor of the House of Representatives on July 11, 2014, Representative Louie Gohmert (R-TX) compared the surge of unaccompanied migrant children to soldiers invading France during World War II—"coming in, in massive invasive waves." (Gohmert)

WORKS CITED

Anderson, Carol. Ferguson Isn't About Black Rage Against Cops. It's White Rage Against Progress. *The Washington Post. The Washington Post*, 2014, August 29. Web. December 2, 2014.

Baca, Damián. *Mestiz@ Scripts, Digital Migrations and the Territories of Writing.* New York: Palgrave, 2008. Print.

Butler, Judith, and Gayatri Chakravorty Spivak. *Who Sings the Nation-State?: Language, Politics, Belonging.* New York and London: Seagull Books, 2007. Print.

Chávez, Leo R. *The Latino Threat: Constructing Immigrants, Citizens, and the Nation.* Stanford, CA: Stanford University Press, 2013. Print.

Cisneros, Josue David. *The Border Crossed Us: Rhetorics of Borders, Citizenship, and Latina/o Identity*, 109–140. Tuscaloosa: U of Alabama Press, 2014. Print.

Flores, William Vincent, and Rina Benmayor. *Latino Cultural Citizenship: Claiming Identity, Space, and Rights.* Boston: Beacon, 1997. Print.

Gohmert, Louie (R-TX). General Speeches. *House Legislative Business.* C-Span. 2014, July 11. Web. November 13, 2014. http://www.c-span.org/video/?320387-1/us-house-legislative-business

Kohn, Sally. When White People Riot. *CNN Opinion.* CNN, 2014, November 20. Web. December 2, 2014.

Licona, Adela C., and Marta Maria Maldonado. The Social Production of Latin@ Visibilities and Invisibilities: Geographies of Power in Small Town America. *Antipode* 46, no. 2 (2014): 517–536. Web. October 28, 2014.

Luibheid, Eithne. *Queer Migrations: Sexuality, US Citizenship, and Border Crossings.* Minneapolis, MN: University of Minneapolis Press, 2005. Print.

Lugo-Lugo, Carmen, and Mary Bloodsworth-Lugo. 'Achor/Terror Babies' and Latina Bodies: Immigration Rhetoric in the 21st Century and the Feminization of Terrorism. *Journal of Interdisciplinary Feminist Thought* 8, no. 1 (2014): 1–21. Print.

Lugones, Maria. Heterosexualism and the Colonial/Modern Gender System. *Hypatia* 22, no. 1 (2007): 186–209. Print.

Medina, Cruz. *Reclaiming Poch@ Pop: Examining the Rhetoric of Cultural Deficiency.* Basingstoke: Palgrave, 2014. Print.

Mignolo, Walter. *Local Histories/Global Designs: Coloniality, Subaltern Knowledges, and Border Thinking.* Princeton, NJ: Princeton University Press, 2000. Print.

Mohanty, Chandra Talpade. *Feminism Without Borders: Decolonizing Theory, Practicing Solidarity.* Durham: Duke UP, 2003. Print.

National Immigrant Youth Alliance. About National Immigrant Youth Alliance. *Facebook.* Facebook, 2000. Web. March 31, 2015.

Nevarez, Griselda. 150 Undocumented Immigrants to Enter US in Border-Crossing Demonstration. *HuffPost Latino Voices,* TheHuffingtonPost.com, 2014, March 11. Web. March 31, 2015.

"No Country for Little Kids." *The Daily Show.* Comedy Central. n.d., September 4. Television.

Park, Haeyoun. Children at the Border. *The New York Times. The New York Times,* 2014, July 14. Web. November 13, 2014.

Sarabia, Heidy. Perpetual Illegality: Results of Border Enforcement and Policies for Mexican Undocumented Migrants in the United States. *Analyses of Social Issues and Public Policy* 12, no. 1 (2012): 49–67. Print.

Schmid, Carol. Challenges at the Periphery of US Citizenship: Birthright Citizenship of Undocumented Immigrants and the Dream Act. In *Citizenship: Practices, Types and Challenges,* ed. Dexter Petty and Clay MacFarland, 47–61. Hauppauge, NY: Nova Science Publishers, 2012. Print.

Somers, Margaret R. *Genealogies of Citizenship: Markets, Statelessness, and the Right to Have Rights.* Cambridge, UK, and New York: Cambridge University Press, 2008. Print.

Somerville, Siobhan. Notes Toward a Queer History of Naturalization. *American Quarterly* 57, no. 3 (2005): 659–675. Print.

Soto, Sandra. *Reading Chican@ Like a Queer: The De-Mastery of Desire.* Austin: University of Texas Press, 2010. Print.

State of Arizona. Cong. Senate. *Senate Bill 1070.* 49th Legislature, 2nd sess. Phoenix, 2010. Print.

United States. Cong. Senate. *Development, Relief, and Education for Alien Minors Act.* 107th Cong. 2nd sess. S. 1291. Washington: GPO, 2001. Proquest Congressional Publications. Web. March 31, 2015.

PART II

Making Texts

CHAPTER 4

History

José Cortez

As rhetoric and composition scholars continue to examine modes of cultural production that have been occluded by the narrative of Western expansion, the role and location of cultural difference within the discipline's historiographic cartographies has become one of the most politically contentious topics. We are bearing witness to a problem, to what Jessica Enoch and David Gold identify as a "methodological moment" (107), and to what LuMing Mao has identified as a "methodological paradox" of writing the other into histories of rhetorics: "[That] is, we have to start somewhere when studying the other—and most likely with concepts or points of reference familiar to us only. We thus risk imposing them on the Other, either forcing an unwanted fit … or espousing a radical divide or incommensurability" (Mao 44).

Indeed, though the discipline has only recently begun to question its geopolitical topology, it is possible now to imagine, as Damián Baca does, a theoretical rupture from previous comparative efforts that carried the baggage of "an enduring Aristotelian syndrome, the rhetorical art of reinventing the cultural Other as a periphery that is declared as such from the colonizing center" ("Rethinking Composition" 230). I under-

J. Cortez (✉)
Department of English, University of Arizona, Tucson, AZ, USA

© The Editor(s) (if applicable) and The Author(s) 2016   49
I.D. Ruiz, R. Sánchez (eds.), *Decolonizing Rhetoric and Composition Studies*, DOI 10.1057/978-1-137-52724-0_4

stand this Aristotelian syndrome to signify foundational or totalizing master narratives of writing that would crystallize it as an a priori object of knowledge. In this chapter, I argue that it is this enduring epistemological syndrome that underpins both traditional and counter-revisionist historiographic accounts of writing.

The political stakes in these conversations are critical, for as recent events concerning the politics of literacy in the state of Arizona demonstrate, the very histories and languages that have been inhabited by Western capitalist expansion have long been the subject of occlusion. As revealed in the controversy surrounding Arizona Senate Bill 2281, which effectively bans ethnic studies in Arizona's public schools, these conversations contain very serious material implications for how people will be able to understand and access both Western and non-Western histories of writing and culture. Indeed, within these conversations lies the possibility for rethinking cultural difference beyond the enduring Aristotelian syndrome. However, in these conversations, the categories of Western and non-Western have more often been assumed than critically interrogated.

What exactly is the relation between the two—what sustains that relation? Is one to be conceived without the other, or does one rely on the ontological guarantee provided by the other? How does accounting for historically occluded voices promote more inclusive histories and theories of rhetorics? In other words, if what is taken as the non-Western is advanced as an authentic rhetorical form—that is, fundamentally different—then what exactly is that fundamental difference and how exactly is it resistant to Western writing? If, as is assumed, there is a difference, how are we to describe this difference and its potential for political reflection?

My project in this chapter is to develop preliminary responses to these questions. I offer a challenge to the means and ends of this Aristotelian syndrome in counter-rhetorical historiography in the Hemispheric American context,[1] and I reflect on the extent to which it can provide a theoretical alternative to dominant historiographical cartographies. To pursue this investigation, I review two approaches to historiography that explore the rhetorical practices of memory, and I consider their political possibilities.

DECOLONIALITY

Recently, scholarship armed with a critical disposition has begun the groundwork on theorizing subaltern agency and cultural difference across regions in the Americas, and Walter Mignolo's decolonial option has emerged as an influential mode of reading in such discussions. In *The Darker Side of the Renaissance: Literacy, Territoriality, and Colonization,* Mignolo introduces an analysis of colonialism in Latin America to conceptualize a relation between writing and cultural identity at the core of political sovereignty in Latin America.[2] Specifically, Mignolo identifies the conceptual linkage of alphabetic technology and literacy with humanity as an ideological thrust of colonialism in Latin America, constituting the pernicious darker side of the Renaissance without which Western Modernity cannot come to bear meaning.

According to Mignolo:

> The early conflict between the Crown and the friars presupposed a theory of the letter and a value-laden educational philosophy claiming the superiority of alphabetic writing and of Western books as a measurement of civilization. The underlying philosophy of writing, the book, and knowledge that we saw in the educational programs of both the Franciscans and the Jesuits was not divorced from the numerous edicts and mandates published by the Crown with the intention of making Castilian available to the Amerindian and, together with teaching how to read and write in Castilian, transmitting Castilian values and manners. It is in this context that, beyond the colonization of native languages or the implementation of a linguistic politics for the expansion of the language of the empire, the theory of the letter also gave rise to a program for the interpretation of culture. (65)

Here, Mignolo frames appeals to colonization as a moralizing, civilizing mission of literacy. It's not so much that the claims of Western writing culture are right or wrong measures for the interpretation of cultures; on the contrary, the narrative of the classical tradition in a genealogy of letters from Greek to Latin to Castilian underpins a comparative method that legitimizes the hierarchical stratification of languages and a hegemonic philosophy of history.

In other words, as European colonialists assumed an ontological linguistic difference, the alphabetic letter became a truth claim for the assumed relation between writing and history.[3] As such, "the belief in the power of the letter to tame the voice, to preserve the glory of the prince and the memories of a nation, and to upgrade the social processes of the Amerindians, who ... had not yet been blessed with the most marvelous human invention [the letter]" framed appeals to colonization as a moral, civilizing mission (Mignolo 37).

Mignolo's work elicits an understanding of how rhetoricians have remained largely unaware of non-Western articulations of language and identity and have therefore hailed non-Western cultures in Latin America into a Eurocentric legacy. As colonialism's narrative presupposed and acted on a prior, ontological difference based in language—that is, that letter and book warranted truth, records, history, and most importantly, sovereignty—this same European "cero-point" remains as the infelicitous coordinates from which alterity is formulated. Mignolo's decolonial project proposes an "epistemic de-linking" from this epistemological and dehumanizing dimension of European colonialism, as, again, the Crown established the epistemological foundations for coloniality on alphabetic literacy: "[M]issionary arguments [were] simple: [Amerindians] do not have alphabetic writing, therefore they cannot have history because for a Renaissance man of the sixteenth century, history was irretrievably linked to alphabetic writing in the Greco-Latin tradition" ("Delinking" 461).

Mignolo's decolonial option distills resistance from an exterior (non-Western) position of colonial difference, assumed to be more accurately representative than the limited locus Eurocentric enunciation. This option, as stated earlier, has proved to be influential in historiographic scholarship interrogating normative Western philosophies of history and engaging the critical rewriting of hegemonic narratives. The decolonial option hinges on this thesis, which drives the indictment of Western theories of writing and rhetoric as provincial, unable alone to serve the needs of writing studies in an increasingly transcultural context.

As with Mignolo, decolonial rhetorics are premised on an ontological difference separating Europe from the Americas and a specific and transgressive condition of subjectivity located in an exterior space from which to speak back to coloniality. This counter-hegemonic mode of critical scholarly practice (delinking scholarly observation and critical practice from the European "cero-point") has taken hold among scholars aiming to assert the sovereignty of non-Western, peripheralized rhetorics as an avenue of radical critical practice.

Baca identifies these colonial legacies in the discipline as the "Eurocentric myth linking the Western Roman alphabet—and eventually English alphabetic literacy—to agency and democracy" ("Rethinking Composition" 230–231). One need look no further than this influence of Western Modernity, which "did play a role in the development of the field's founding image of the writer. And attached to that figure was a corresponding notion of ultimate sovereign agency" (Sánchez 236). Baca's solution is to look toward *mestiz@* rhetorics, which revise dominant colonial metanarratives (including the rectilinear East–West civilizing narrative of literacy on which Rhetoric and Writing Studies rest) and create new literacies by hybridizing pre-Colombian and contemporary modes of semiosis to create inventions between colonial oppositions. These rhetorical practices—theoretically underpinned by Gloria Anzaldúa's *mestiza* consciousness—promote decolonial translations and revisions of colonial narratives and global designs. Cristina Ramirez's study of mestiza rhetors makes an anticolonial appeal to *mestizaje* as an originary racial difference that allowed women subalterns to enter into hegemony from subalternity. One could cite other examples of decolonial historiographical scholarship premised on an exteriority to Western Modernity.

However, when the grounds of this critical position are critically interrogated, one finds yet again that decolonial historiographical scholarship has failed to enact a theoretical break from the enduring Aristotelian syndrome. At the core of decolonial appeals to hybridity, one finds a troubling question. As Abraham Acosta writes: "[I]f by categorically distinguishing between indigenous and Western forms of hybridity, based exclusively on the requirement for pure categories, has [one] not just reproduced the conditions of purity/impurity that 'indigenous' hybridity claims to be able to do without?" (42). As Acosta's question reveals, the appeal to non-Western hybridity as an a priori, postrepresentational position also derives from a logic of purity. It represents Aristotelianism in the form of a cross-cultural, nonrepresentational critical disposition that tries to locate subaltern speech on its own terms. It also reveals the rhetorical tradition through such an appeal to cultural authenticity and reproduces the claims and narratives of cultural difference that (re)establish (neo)colonial forms of hegemony.[4]

History is better understood in relation, neither to past events, nor to present observations but rather as a discursive threshold that obtains substance between mutually exclusive modes of remembering. Resisting Western exceptionalism through historiographic reclamation of a reverse-ethnocentric narrative is analogically parallel to the mode of colonial memory that frames Amerindian cultural production as inherently aphilosophical, ahistorical, and subhuman.[5] The task for critical historiographic reflection today lies in tracing how hegemonic rationality is served by reconstituting Latin America and the peripheries of Western Modernity (including those occluded interperipheries of the metropoles) as the non-Western outsides of Western Modernity's inside—even and especially in the name of colonial difference as the basis for political resistance. For it is "the limits of the inside-outside relation itself (neither/nor) and … the continuous threat of indistinction upon which such dualities are always founded and which are kept hidden from view" (Acosta 73).

SUBALTERNITY

In contrast, the framework of subalternity proposes that the subaltern is a constitutive subject-effect as a deferred representation that will remain heterogenous to the intellectual. For by definition, the subaltern is conceived as such because it cannot achieve the state and cannot emerge into hegemonic representation (Spivak 16). For Acosta, systematic misreadings of Spivak's notion of subalternity "as the impetus for the political relation rather than as the discursive effect of the discipline's complicity in the persistent constitution of the Other as the Self's shadow" underpins a postrepresentational exteriority that assumes subaltern agency to be a radical exteriority from which to revise asymmetrical power relations (52). It is in this invocation of subalternity that Acosta critiques orality as unmediated subaltern speech and demonstrates the paradoxes of building theories of resistance from identity (*mestizaje*) as an inherently resistant and less-hegemonic condition. A similar misreading is ongoing in rhetorical studies, where a metaleptic understanding of subalternity (on whether the subaltern can speak and whether the intellectual is listening to such speech) occludes the potential for radically rethinking hegemonic–subaltern power relations.

Lynda Walsh's take on subaltern studies scholarship, for example, proposes a new version of critical hybridity "that would yield a traceable account of the rhetorical and political agency of specific textual mixtures of discourse traditions" (393). This conclusion emerges from her misapprehension of postcoloniality's subjective elements, which I cite here at length:

An example of this translation problem can be seen in Anjali Prabhu's study. … She reads hybrid novels and memoirs, most of them written in French, the language of the colonizer of Mauritius and La Réunion. By reading these memoirs, the oppressed population of Mauritius can "write itself into the national context" and even in some cases enact "revolutionary moments" (92). Expecting serious social agency to derive from books only 3 [%] of the population can read or write seems optimistic in the extreme. But this is the typical formula by which social agency is generated in postcolonial theory: the subaltern will read a hybrid memoir and identify with the author, creating a psychological perception of solidarity with the author and other subaltern readers. This perception of solidarity can turn into actual social solidarity and thus, potentially, found political action ... or, by similar logic, the subaltern will write a hybrid identity that releases him/her from the gaze of the colonizer and opens up a psychological space for individual political agency. .... These formulae are always stated as self-efficacious, unsupported by any data from actual reading events. (98)

She continues this critique by noting a consensual failure, in poststructuralist accounts at least, to locate agency:

[P]ost-structuralist accounts like Spivak's or Anzaldúa's define agency somewhere in between (in scale, at least), as taking a subject position that defies categorization by the dominant political regime, thus creating the preconditions for solidarity with other "excessive" individuals. A lack of consensus about where to locate hybrid agency in postcolonial studies has certainly contributed to difficulties in demonstrating it. (Walsh, 400)

Here Walsh critiques hybridity on a misreading of the workings of representation in the concept of hybridity. Although Anzaldúa certainly can be said to initiate a search for subaltern agency as a subject in-between subject formations, Spivak describes subalternity as a persistent series of failures and, ultimately, as a constitutive category that retroactively takes the subject-effect to be a guarantee of its reasoning.

Maritza Cardenas, for example, maintains that subject categories of Latinx and Latin American are sustained through the exclusion of US Central Americans: "Central American-Americaness is more than just a state of marginality, for it is not simply that Central American-American subjects and cultures exist at the periphery of discourses of American and Latino cultural citizenship, but rather that they are produced in and through those spaces of exclusion" (28). It is not simply that subalterns exist in the colonial peripheries, but instead that subalterns are constitutively produced through peripheral spaces. This understanding (along with Walsh's assessment that critical hybridity lacks the capacity to locate, generate, and predict transnationally hybrid rhetorical production) indicates that the ability to account for the political agency of specific textual mixtures remains elusive.

The same is the case for Christian Weisser, for whom subalternity assumes an ability for categorical self-representation—the potential for subalterns to know and speak from the self. This is critical to Weisser's argument in two ways. First, in order to explain how subaltern groups resist the discursive silencing efforts of hegemony, the definition of subalternity is wrapped irreducibly into the definition of "publics," who must "intend to convince others to think or act differently" to be considered publics (611). In other words, subaltern speech is assumed to be public and registerable, for subaltern counterpublics "seek to write themselves back into public conversations rather than detach from them," implying a purpose of "inclusion rather than separation, since they intend to make themselves heard" (610–11). Second, Weisser's concept of subaltern self-representation is taken to explain how "counterpublics [consist] of diverse peoples focused upon common goals, developing alternative rhetorical conventions that [challenge] and [question] the ideological norms of dominant publics" (618).

To account for the heterogeneity of subaltern self-representation and the disruptions they are taken to speak, Weisser reads the "dialogue surrounding issues, rather than the identity of the population that is engaging in the discourse" (618). Ultimately, what this means is that reframing subalternity as a concept of rhetorical publics (from a conception of representative identity to a conception of nonrepresentative "locus of diverse publics") is taken to develop insight into emerging subaltern counterpublics and the heterogeneous modes in which they "shift rhetorical strategies to highlight their message, call into question the ideological constraints of dominant publics, and better meet the needs of their subaltern constituents" (616).

Arizona HB2281

Disciplinary reflection about ethnoracial difference in the state of Arizona often describes an anti-Latinx or anti-Mexican political milieu (see Martinez; Medina; Medina and Martinez), and given that Arizona Senate Bill 2281 directly targets Mexican American Studies and followed on the heels of SB 1070, it can be of little surprise that thinking about cultural difference in this context continues to be known through a Latinx–Anglo binary grid of intelligibility. Anna Ochoa O'Leary et al. summarize one side of this grid, asserting that "legislative policies such as HB 2281—not the MAS courses—create racial division and feelings of resentment in Arizona. HB 2281 is ideologically motivated legislation designed to keep Other people of color from recognizing their commonalities, developing coalitions, and creating stronger democracy in Arizona" (11).

There can be little doubt that the legislation in question represents the latest instance in a long and pernicious effort to maintain institutional ethnoracial inequality in the area. In addition, as far as one can tell from this claim, racial hegemony in the state is to be understood as emanating asymmetrically from the sovereign state itself. It also can be concluded that political work therefore would focus on overturning the flow of power from its source in the state.

Alternatively, when HB 2281 was passed into law in 2010, Arizona Attorney General Tom Horne gave the following rationale in support of the bill:

> People are individuals, not exemplars of racial groups. What is important about people is what they know, what they can do, their ability to appreciate beauty, their character, and not what race into which they are born. They are entitled to be treated that way. It is fundamentally wrong to divide students up according to their racial group, and teach them separately. (1)

As one can easily read the neoconservative subtext operating within Horne's justification, it becomes clear that he seems unaware—or perhaps hyperaware—of a more essential hegemonic claim. Horne's frame of equality signals a deadlock grounded in an understanding of racial belonging. His statement enlists the perception of race not only to authorize an already-entrenched ethnoracial hierarchy but also to reinscribe the form through which this hierarchy is established.

When positioned against each other, these arguments form co-constitutively opposing appeals that hinge on a perception of race: both claim that dividing people by racial identification is fundamentally wrong. As such, if one cannot so easily determine the true form of racial partition and equal belonging, a deadlock of mutually exclusive hegemonic claims begins to take shape.

The threshold binding hegemonic and counter-hegemonic rhetoric in the Arizona context as co-constitutive yet mutually exclusive programs for achieving equality, then, cannot be solved simply by enlisting identity as the category for reversing one position in favor of the other. And although the full outcome of the laws within the larger scope of migration has yet to be seen, it is evident in this deadlock that the grid of intelligibility along the US–Mexico border in Arizona—indeed, our very understanding of the political textures of this space—has already been established.

One such rhetorical consequence of the passage of both laws has been, as Acosta asserts, a reflexive identification of one ethnoracial group as the "subhegemonic cultural minority in whose name, history, and identity the conflict takes exclusive shape," adding that "what we are seeing here, in the name of diversity, is an appeal to the logic of hegemony—the very one used against the Mexican/Mexican American community—that subsumes and subordinates the interests of other groups to the interests of the most populous of them" (104). Again, this legislation represents yet another episode of historical state oppression against the sizable Mexican American community. It is clear that Mexican American Latinxs will not be the only ethnocultural minority group that will be affected.

In case we are to believe that what is happening represents a single deviation of public education and hegemonic "whiteness"—a single instantiation of neoliberal state activity—this historical moment instead reveals precisely what the systems of public education are designed to produce: a homogeneous space for able-bodied, economically advantaged students to maintain and reproduce a highly exclusive system of power-knowledge that will yield ever more exclusion and privilege. We can identify this as systemic whiteness.

This case provides the grounds for rethinking the discipline's historiographic cartography not from yet another Aristotelian framework, which is revealed as both the tradition and its resistance together in a system of political antagonism, but from the textuality of subalternity. If resistant rhetorics are advanced on topoi of exteriority—much as the decolonial option is built on the notion that Latin America expresses an authentically non-Western voice—then resistance rhetorics risk becoming chiral enterprises of the oppression they dispute.

Therefore, what's at stake in this is a discursive order that affects all groups, and as such,

> … a response informed by, inclusive of, and in the non-name of All obtains now as a most critical and historical imperative: that regardless of population size or history in the area, every minority group has the right to assert the right to representation anywhere—even against the most traditional and predominant groups among them (Acosta 241)

The lesson to be learned, for rhetorical historiography, not in the name of *Latinidad*, but "in the non-name of All" is that no groups are exceptional, and if that decoloniality as a theory for developing critical historiographic reflection is to hold water, it might be best understood as a practice of reading for the de-exceptionalism of all groups laying claim.

I find it frightening, yet nonetheless urgent, that historiographical disruptions to hegemonic orders of meaning and writing may now require one to subvert one's own cultural allegiances. In other words, historiographic appeals to hegemonic representation in ethnic studies on the ontological basis of the growing number and visibility of minorities occludes our thinking beyond hegemonic orders of meaning and value. In this sense, to decolonize the irreducibly bound rectilinear histories of rhetoric and writing would require one to de-exceptionalize and render arbitrary all dichotomies in an effort to claim that the historical constitution of the social text can be otherwise.

NOTES

1. I use the term "Americas" to refer to scholarship dedicated to studying the representations of the signification, cultural production, and social antagonism resulting from the spread of colonialism in North, Central, and South America. Derived from Baca, *Mestiz@ Scripts*; Baca and Villanueva; Cushman, *The Cherokee Syllabary*; Olson, *Constitutive Visions*.

2. Readers will recognize this idea in Baca's claim for "why the Eurocentric myth linking the Western Roman alphabet—and eventually, English alphabetic literacy—to agency, and democracy can potentially mean little" ("Rethinking" 231).

3. Consider, for example, that the *New Georgia Encyclopedia*, an open-access, web encyclopedia maintained by the state of Georgia, identifies *Sequoyah* as "the only member of an illiterate group in human history to have single-handedly devised a successful system of writing" ("Sequoyah").

4. It is important to remember that in critiquing recovery efforts, I am in no way discounting these historiographic practices. Instead, my interest is in continuing to reflect on the questions posed by this form and to expand ever more inclusive practices of rhetorical inquiry and reflection. The idea offered here for rhetorical historiography in the Americas is not to disavow rhetoric, history, or any

Western concepts deemed Eurocentric. Instead, what is at stake here is rhetoric's unacknowledged relationship with the legacies of coloniality in the Americas, what that relationship means conceptually, and the possibilities for developing critical practices equipped to read for the conceptual disruption of hegemonic orders.

5. Derived from Angela Haas, who argues that race and place are important components of technical communications research and pedagogy through a wide-ranging review of scholarship on race, rhetoric, and technology. Haas defines the framework for a graduate course titled "Race, Rhetoric, and Technology" that aims to
. . . decolonize the Western rhetorical canon and epistemology … for writing faculty who teach with technology to be more cognizant of the colonial constructs that we may inadvertently reinscribe in our classrooms, and … for our discipline to make a cultural turn and to re-theorize our theories and practices as assemblages of 'contested, localized, conjunctural knowledges' that must be put into dialogue. (295)
Her methods are described as follows:

In brief, decolonial methodologies and pedagogies serve to (a) redress colonial influences on perceptions of people, literacy, language, culture, and community and the relationships therein and (b) support the coexistence of cultures, languages, literacies, memories, histories, places, and spaces—and encourage respectful and reciprocal dialogue between and across them. As part of this pedagogy, I interrogate how colonialism and imperialism have informed our understandings of race, rhetoric, and technology, including, but not limited to, how we have historically been informed about race via technology and technical communication and which races have been considered technically and technologically superior and inferior—and why. Thus, my pedagogical and curricular approach both builds on and extends feminist scholarship on technical communication and Grobman's (1999) call to employ multicultural perspectives in our pedagogy in order to transform our classrooms to contact zones. (297)

There is no doubt that race, place, and coloniality are vitally important aspects to theorizing ever more inclusive pedagogical practices. But ultimately, Haas does not provide an example of the theoretical principles at work that would delink students or theory from the colonial matrix. This Western–non-Western binary relies on an understanding of cultural difference that is dialectically opposed to the Eurocentric locus of enunciation, but not necessarily exterior to it.

WORKS CITED

Acosta, Abraham. *Thresholds of Illiteracy: Theory, Latin America, and the Crisis of Resistance*. New York: Fordham University Press, 2014. Print.

Baca, Damián. *Mestiz@ Scripts, Digital Migrations, and the Territories of Writing*. New York: Palgrave, 2008. Print.

Baca, Damián. Rethinking Composition, Five Hundred Years Later. *JAC* 29 (2013): 229–242. Print.

Baca, Damián, and Victor Villanueva, eds. *Rhetorics of the Americas: 3114 BCE to 2012 CE*. New York: Palgrave, 2010. Print.

Bahri, Deepika. Terms of Engagement: Postcolonialism, Transnationalism, and Composition Studies. *JAC* 18 (1998): 29–44. Print.

Cushman, Ellen. *The Cherokee Syllabary: Writing the People's Perseverance*. Norman: University of Oklahoma Press, 2011. Print.

Cushman, Ellen. Wampum, Sequoyan, and Story: Decolonizing the Digital Archive. *College English* 76 (2013): 115–135. Print.

Enoch, Jessica, and David Gold. Introduction: Seizing the Methodological Moment: The Digital Humanities and Historiography in Rhetoric and Composition. *College English* 76 (2013): 105–114. Print.

Haas, Angela M. Race, Rhetoric, and Technology: A Case Study of Decolonial Technical Communication Theory, Methodology, and Pedagogy. *Journal of Business and Technical Communication* 26 (2012): 277–310. Print.

Mao, LuMing. Writing the Other into Histories of Rhetorics: Theorizing the Art of Recontextualization. In *Theorizing Histories of Rhetoric*, ed. Michelle Ballif, 41–57. Carbondale: Southern Illinois UP, 2012. Print.

Martinez, Aja Y. 'The American Way': Resisting the Empire of Force and Color-Blind Racism. *College English* 71 (2009): 584–595. Print.

Medina, Cruz. Nuestros Refranes: Culturally Relevant Writing in Tucson High Schools. *Reflections: Public Rhetoric, Civic Writing, and Service Learning* 13 (2013): 52–75. Print.

Medina, Cruz, and Aja Y. Martinez. Contexts of Lived Realities in SB 1070 Arizona: A Response to Asenas and Johnson's "Economic Globalization and the 'Given Situation.'" *Present Tense* 4 (2015): n. pag. Print.

Mignolo, Walter D. *The Darker Side of the Renaissance: Literacy, Territoriality, and Colonization*. Ann Arbor: University of Michigan P, 1995. Print.

Olson, Christa J. *Constitutive Visions: Indigeneity and Commonplaces of National Identity in Republican Ecuador.* University Park: Penn State UP, 2014. Print.

Ramirez, Cristina. Forging a Mestiza Rhetoric: Mexican Women Journalists' Role in the Construction of a National Identity. *College English* 71 (2009): 606–629. Print.

Sánchez, Raúl. Outside the Text: Retheorizing Empiricism and Identity. *College English* 74 (2012): 234–246. Print.

Spivak, Gayatri Chakravorty. Subaltern Studies: Deconstructing Historiography. *Selected Subaltern Studies,* ed. Ranajit Guja and Gayatri Chakravorty Spivak, 4–32. New York: Oxford UP, 1988. Print.

Wadley, Ted. Sequoyah (ca. 1770-ca. 1840). *New Georgia Encyclopedia.* Web. January 13, 2015.

Walsh, Lynda. Accountability : Towards a Definition of Hybridity for Scholars of Transnational Rhetorics. *Rhetorica* 30 (2012): 392–431. Print.

Weisser, Christian R. Subaltern Counterpublics and the Discourse of Protest. *JAC* 28 (2013): 608–620. Print.

CHAPTER 5

Code Switching

José Cano

In a course on composition pedagogy, I wrote an academic essay employing code-switching practices: mixing Spanish with English. That essay used words, sentences, and major portions of paragraphs from both languages. The practice itself was the end-goal; there was no need to revise it all into Standard Written English. Because code switching prevails in discussions about Latinxs and their language practices, and because it has caught my attention as a pedagogical approach, I wanted to have firsthand experience as a student before applying it to others. It proved to be an interesting writing experience: the rhetorical situation became more complicated than I anticipated.

I decided to to write an essay discussing pedagogical approaches to writing instruction in a voice that I typically used with a limited number of friends and colleagues in and out of academic contexts. I couldn't remember when, or if, I had ever written anything that mixed Spanish and English. It's easy to speak that way, but it's a completely different experience to write it, since there's time to think about those rhetorical choices and their effects on others. I knew the professor would understand the text—she knew Spanish. But sharing it with others in the class might be

J. Cano (✉)
Department of English, Pace High School, Brownsville, TX, USA

© The Editor(s) (if applicable) and The Author(s) 2016
I.D. Ruiz, R. Sánchez (eds.), *Decolonizing Rhetoric and Composition Studies*, DOI 10.1057/978-1-137-52724-0_5

problematic because I did not know all of their linguistic backgrounds. So the larger rhetorical situation still loomed.

In rhetoric and composition, few scholars discuss Latinxs' code-switching practices. When they (or their students) do, they seem to focus on Gloria Anzaldúa's *Borderlands/La Frontera: The New Mestiza*. In her writing, Anzaldúa performs incredible code-switching feats that transcend multiple boundaries. But without further readings or observations of similar situations, Latinxs and others may learn a one-dimensional conception of the practice. In my own essay, I did not want the text simply to mimic Anzaldúa's discussion and example of code switching. And I worried about recreating a specific stereotype through certain practices. These factors and others comprised the larger rhetorical situation that quickly complicated writing the essay. But I wrote it anyway, and the experience focused my thinking on the practice of code switching. In the end, I concluded that as much as it champions the mixing of languages, code-switching also requires a form of bilingual literacy in English and Spanish.

CODE SWITCHING AND BILINGUAL LITERACY

In fact, I believe code-switching can't be discussed apart from bilingual literacy. Yet, as Jaime Armin Mejía writes:

> One could search in vain to find significant studies in rhetoric and composition journals discussing particular writing problems and rhetorical situations facing bilinguals, such as Texas Mexican college students. One could expand research to include all Mexican Americans, or more broadly still, Hispanic students, yet one would find little if anything of any significance or relevance to teaching bilingual and bicultural critical literacy. (174)

Mejía points toward an area that rhetoric and composition continuously fails to address in research and practice. And although I want to discuss code switching, I begin with bilingualism because code switching's end-goal should be bilingual critical literacy. By itself, code switching—the mixing of English and Spanish—only accounts for a fraction of a bilingual student's potential rhetorical repertoire. Bilingual critical literacy requires further development through its continued practice.

My perspective on code switching does not apply indiscriminately to every postsecondary institution in the United States. Certain regions and institutions lend themselves to the formulation and application of approaches that seriously consider Latinxs' material and rhetorical situations. One such region is the Rio Grande Valley, and Rolando Hinojosa provides a sense of its dynamics. In "This Writer's Sense of Place," he explains his creation of realistic characters in his fictional work and his rhetorical choices for their linguistic practices:

> When the characters stayed in the Spanish-speaking milieu or society, the Spanish language worked well, and then it was in the natural order of things that English made its entrance when the characters strayed or found themselves in Anglo institutions; in cases where both cultures would come into contact, both languages were used, and I would employ both, and where one and only one would do, I would follow that as well. (15)

Here Hinojosa describes some of the dynamics of the Rio Grande Valley. He later adds that "generational and class differences also dictated not only usage but which language [to use] as well" (15). Race, class, history, generational status, and other characteristics factor in to create intricate rhetorical and material situations for people of this area.

In particular, Hinojosa's attention to generational differences corroborates a survey conducted by the Pew Hispanic Center on bilingualism. The report finds that by the third generation, Latinxs do tend to lose their first language and adopt English, but not as "comprehensively, rapidly and readily as scholars suggest" ("Bilingualism" 5). Another report finds that as Spanish-speaking proficiency falters, there is also a decline in reading proficiency (Taylor, Lopez, Martínez, and Velasco). From these findings, we might conclude that Spanish writing ability declines, or perhaps is never acquired. What role does code switching play in this trend toward monolingual English?

Rosaura Sánchez weighs in on this topic. In *Chicano Discourse: Sociohistoric Perspectives*, she claims that code-switching occurs because of language attrition. She points out that older generations maintain Spanish while younger generations use English as their native language, and she notes that the "intermediate step is often code-switching" (142). Sánchez reminds readers of an important feature of US Spanish-speaking communities: "the dominant and literate language will gradually eliminate the subordinate language" (142).

Because English functions as the language of literacy in most spheres in the United States, people may not see a need for Spanish literacy, so it vanishes. While this process of Spanish erasure transpires, code switching may occur. I'm not suggesting that this practice poses any challenges to the students who exercise it, nor am I promoting a deficit perspective to its study, but I am emphasizing that as generations pass, many individuals lose their language.

By championing a traditional view of code switching, do scholars and educators unintentionally promote the inevitable loss of Spanish? I believe the answer is no. In certain situations, where students have already lost most of their Spanish speaking, reading, and writing abilities, this approach asks them to exercise a language with which they may not be intimately familiar. In states where vocal opposition to this language exists, a traditional approach also defies such discriminatory practices.

On the other hand, if students possess considerable bilingual proficiency, a traditional code-switching approach may not prompt them to develop a more extensive rhetorical repertoire. Even though they can showcase their ability to infuse Spanish into their written English or vice versa, it's more impressive if they can write in Spanish alone, given the circumstances of language loss in the United States. This "Spanish-only" is a practice that stems from a decolonial perspective, as I will explain later. Grandparents, parents, educators, and students themselves make active choices in an effort to maintain, develop, or acquire Spanish. They choose to use it in different spheres of their lives: watching TV, interacting with family members, attending religious institutions, enrolling in bilingual or Spanish classes, reading newspapers, and so on.

A Brief View

Before proceeding, I want to acknowledge various outdated beliefs about language practices, which I try not to reproduce: the belief that language can or should be pure, that one language is superior to another, and that code switching is an inferior language practice. Despite being outdated, these views are so prevalent that scholars can never ignore them when constructing feasible and applicable writing alternatives for Latinxs. Because of misunderstanding and lack of information, people have assumed Latinxs who practice code switching are deficient in linguistic ability and rhetorical agility.

Guadalupe Valdés Fallis, for example, notes that linguist Uriel Weinreich "defines *insufficient adherence to language* as an abnormal proneness to switching attributed to persons who in early childhood were addressed indiscriminately in both languages by the same familiar speakers" as a cause for code-switching (878). In other words, Weinreich suggests that parents, friends, and community members who code-switch hinder children's linguistic development because they encourage abnormal language practices. This view of code switching presents an antiquated but persistent view, which students sometimes share.

In her study, "Spanish-English Code-Switching among US Latinos," Almeida Jacqueline Toribio investigates the attitudes and code-switching practices of several Spanish–English bilinguals who represent a larger pool of participants. Toribio finds that "rather than subject themselves to the stereotype associated with those who engage in code-switching, these speakers, typified by Rosalba [one of her participants], renounce its use altogether" (115). Toribio explains that Latinxs' own negative perceptions of code-switching heavily influences its ideological and practical components; some students refuse altogether to mix languages, so as not to fall prey to negative stereotypes.

Fortunately, academic perception of this matter has shifted significantly. For decades scholars have worked hard to reframe code switching. In the 1970s, Valdés Fallis began exploring the code-switching practices of Latinx. After analyzing several poems, she found that "the bilingual poet, as opposed to the poet who confines himself to one language, can at any point in the poem choose to foreground in the language, which to him, offers the greatest possibilities" (884). Valdés Fallis thus frames Latinxs as active participants in their code-switching practices, not as victims unable to function in either language.

In a more contemporary text, Rosina Lippi-Green advocates for acknowledging and embracing code switching as an academically viable rhetorical practice. Lippi-Green counters the prevalent view: "To call code-switching *Spanglish* in a dismissive way is just another subordination method with a long history: to deny a language and its people a distinct name is to refuse to acknowledge them" (original emphasis; 281). More closely aligned to rhetoric and composition, Michelle Hall Kells contests the attitudes that surround code switching and its users. She affirms that negative beliefs about it "fail to account for the fact that code-switching is a universal phenomenon of language contact" (27), which means that educators should not see Latinxs' own code-switching practices as detrimental to their development of literacy.

Rhetoric and composition emphasizes code switching as a subversive approach to writing because the field itself has always been extremely focused on written English. Code switching requires the ability to write in a single code (English or Spanish) but also the ability to switch to the other a single rhetorical act. Current Latinx students in writing classes can more easily write in English or mix languages, but rarely can they write in Spanish alone. Asking them to write monolingually in Spanish would not deny the language mixing that inherently occurs wherever people with different languages or dialects interact. After all, that is how language evolves; it is picked up, thrown around, and mixed up. But for bilingual Latinxs, a traditional conception of code switching occludes the fact that English continues to develop while Spanish vanishes, at least for these individuals. Although championing the mixing of Spanish and English advanced a particular agenda during the 1970s, the more ambitious goal is academic bilingual critical literacy, which has already gained a foothold in rhetoric and composition.

Students can develop English and Spanish literacy skills simultaneously. In *"Más allá del inglés,"* Isis Artze-Vega, Elizabeth I. Doud, and Belkys Torres describe a bilingual approach to composition that includes course components foregrounding bilinguals and their rhetorical choices. They state that "Latinos/as often are encouraged to become monolingual, yet we hope that our approach conveys an appreciation for bilingualism in the face of, and indeed to work against, societal oppression" (102). The authors say that it is possible to practice a bilingual approach because students still develop analytical and rhetorical skills (100).

Daniel Villa agrees that "students falling anywhere along the bilingual continuum who have rarely or never written Spanish regularly produce well-organized, logically constructed essays in the language using sophisticated argument structures," and he points toward English literacy as a foundation for this outcome (90). In essence, rhetoric and composition has the capability to build on the linguistic skills that will enable students to write in two distinct codes without switching from one to another in the same text. Attempting not to switch codes within a single text may sound like linguistic homogeneity and purity, but it isn't. It simply challenges a very tangible reality, one where students lose their spoken Spanish within a few generations of being in the United States and rarely acquire formal written literacy in this same language.

This brief glimpse of code switching considers the difficult work undertaken to establish a perspective that acknowledges the rhetorical agility and skillfulness that bilinguals bring to this complicated linguistic practice. Even though traditional code switching practices still require attention,

Spanish and English literacies as separate languages pose a useful and worthy pursuit in the education of Latinxs.

CODE SWITCHING FROM A DECOLONIAL APPROACH

Emma Pérez delineates an innovative approach to the field of history and writing with her concept of the "decolonial imaginary." She asks readers to consider the past as a "colonial imaginary" that has only allowed one side of the story of the Americas to be told and heard, to the exclusion of people with different genders, sexualities, and races (5). Pérez's decolonial imaginary stems from a colonial past but works at "decolonizing otherness where all identities are at work in one way or another" (7). This approach produces a different system of thought that foregrounds silenced or unheard voices, challenging colonial legacies.

These legacies exclude and erase languages. For example, Pérez asserts that Malintzin Tenapal's "words were not transcribed by anyone who may have listened at a time when orality was the method of passing tales to the next generation" (xv). This situation closely parallels bilingual Latinxs in writing classes. These students possess oral abilities in Spanish but rarely write out their own texts in Spanish. Their writing is typically in English, which may exclude some of their histories, identities, and experiences.

Keith Gilyard provides a definition of code switching that prompts a larger conversation about its study and practice. He uses a TV set as a metaphor to explain that individuals don't switch from channel to channel; instead, the TV set itself decides which channels will appear. After this depiction, Gilyard looks at the term *code* and defines it as follows:

> [A] culturally inscribed and circumscribed but ultimately inner-driven strategy based on an individual's interpretation of social-linguistic situations. It follows that code switching, if we hold on to that term a little longer, is not a simple skill for hopping from channel to channel but a complex choice made, whether consciously or subconsciously, relative to a culture-wide system of meaning. (116–117)

Gilyard's definition of code switching and what it entails opens venues for viewing it from a decolonial perspective. His TV set metaphor identifies a "culture-wide system of meaning." This system helps create the overarching rhetorical situation for individuals in US education systems. For the most part, these education systems teach students in the English language and promote an Anglophone approach to literacy studies.

Gilyard's definition of code and code switching places individuals in positions where they possess the ability to read their own situations and to make complex rhetorical choices. From Pérez's decolonial imaginary, this culture-wide system of meaning functions as the colonial force imposing its linguistic, historical, and rhetorical practices on others. Those who refuse to switch to the right channels, or codes, are muted or not heard. Still, Gilyard leaves ample room for individuals to act in their respective rhetorical and material situations, which presents them as active agents in their rhetorical practices.

In addition to Gilyard, Latinxs in rhetoric and composition also have employed code switching in writings that help expand its range and further establish a decolonial perspective. Juan C. Guerra's "From Code-Segregation to Code-Switching to Code-Meshing" begins with a paragraph in Spanish, switches between English and Spanish in the following paragraph, and ultimately exercises English-only for the rest of its delivery. Reflecting on his own use of languages, Guerra states "[t] hat choice [using academic conference English], to me, is what code-switching is all about. We read our audience, and we perform in a way that reflects the dynamic tension between a clueless conformity and a relentless rebellion. It's never perfect, but it works" (37). He describes reading the rhetorical situation, looking at his own options, and performing in such a way as to produce favorable outcomes for him and his audience. Guerra considers his entire text and use of conference academic English an act of code switching.

For Latinxs, code switching, in an extremely rhetorical sense, engages creating or reading an audience, looking for the available linguistic options, and executing them in an effective method. Guerra challenges the notion of code switching as simply mixing languages in a single text. In the same way that Pérez puts forth a Chicana subjectivity to "foreground gender as an inaugural category of analysis" (7), Guerra establishes a bilingual Latinx's subjectivity as the frame of reference. His observations about code-switching practices reflect a linguistic reality for Latinxs.

Guerra's approach further expands the study and scope of code switching because researchers now have to consider why a bilingual Latinx chooses to employ a single language even with knowledge of two. This kind of code switching is continuous and not a mechanism that can be turned on and off at will. In other words, bilingual Latinxs are *never not* code-switching. These languages exist in specific material and rhetorical situations that need to be considered and included in any concept and practice of code switching. Guerra succeeds in switching the perspective from a monolingual view of code switching to one that positions the bilingual writer at the fore.

To develop code-switching from a decolonial perspective, it's important to specify the acquisition and use of Spanish as much as English, and we must also include the development of critical literacy skills when exercising either language. In *Zines in Third Space: Radical Cooperation and Borderlands Rhetoric*, Adela C. Licona examines zines created by feminists who engage with discussions of racialization, sexualization, class, and gender. In these zines, Licona finds and analyzes code-switching practices. Although she views code switching as "a change in language within a given context," Licona writes that "third-space tactics and borderlands rhetorics are often comprised of code switching or bilingualism as a means of representing lived experiences and thereby resisting limits of dominant discourses" (52–53). For Latinxs, Licona's perspective on code switching embodies more than the switching of languages in a single text because her elaboration unveils that code-switching practices arise from lived experiences.

Latinxs' lived experiences challenge colonial forces that position specific practices and ways of living as unwanted, thus invalidating them in academic realms. These experiences provide an opening to include various factors such as language, race, ethnicity, class, sexual orientation, and gender into the concept of code switching. For example, a researcher now has to consider how these specific factors help create the context in which people engage in code-switching. Licona adds: "As a practice, code switching demonstrates a commitment to the value of lived experience and the validity and import of the (allegedly) impure in nondominant contexts" (53)—that is, it moves beyond a linguistic practice. To Licona, code switching commits itself to advancing the varied perspectives of Latinxs. Through this inclusion of lived experiences, Latinxs' code-switching practices come to light through their own lens, and she asks others to recognize it as such.

In an interview with Andrea Lunsford, Gloria Anzaldúa discusses her own use of code switching. Responding to Lunsford's question on mixing styles, she states: "Well other Chicanas were mixing Spanglish in poetry, but not in theory, not in academic writing. And I think of styles as trying to recover a childhood place where you code switch" (21). By focusing on Spanglish as a code-switching practice, Anzaldúa substantiates that bilinguals only code-switch when they mix languages or dialects. She implies that bilingual Latinxs don't use it when adhering to a single language or dialect, whether a dialect of Spanish or English. However, Anzaldúa also writes: "But I think that what I was trying to do by code-switching was to inject some of my history and some of my identity into this text that White people were going to read or Black people were going to read or Native American people were going to read" (21).

Here Anzaldúa explains that code switching means the inclusion of her history and identity into her writing. This inclusion performs a vital function for code-switching practices from a decolonial perspective because it allows consideration of different identities (or perhaps, identifications) and histories from the perspective of people of color and other silenced minorities. The history of Latinxs vastly differs from the history of the Anglos, so infusing Latinx history into writing engages specific topics for performing certain rhetorical maneuvers. Anzaldúa succeeds in injecting her text with her own identity by writing from certain positions and speaking back to a colonial force by constructing her argument with constant reference to the female body, indigenous histories, and linguistic diversity. Although Anzaldúa champions the mixing of languages, she accomplishes much more than just bringing in Spanish, English, and Tex-Mex, among other dialects. Anzaldúa's awareness of her audience brings an ethical component to the application of code switching. Her ability to switch should enable her to reach a wider audience rather than restrict her writing to a single sphere.

Anzaldúa and other Latinxs need the support of White, Black, Native American, and other minority groups to share and listen to create some type of change to a colonial force that affects all races and genders in different ways. In essence, Anzaldúa and Licona understand that lived experiences, histories, and identities are embedded into code-switching practices, and these practices should promote the perspectives of their Latinx practitioners because their voices have gone unheard for too long. Nevertheless, they don't champion a Latinx perspective at the expense of silencing others, which would recreate the same colonial approach.

Licona's and Anzaldúa's descriptions of code switching work to enhance its definition and scope, fitting it within a decolonial perspective. Pérez writes that "the decolonial imaginary in Chicana/o history is a theoretical tool for uncovering the hidden voices of Chicanas that have been relegated to silences, to passivity" (xvi). These two writers consider the impact of experiences, histories, and identities on the understanding and application of code-switching practices. They provide a previously silenced voice in academic contexts and have emphasized that this practice engages more than simply switching between languages. People who code-switch deploy knowledge and rhetorical agility in their linguistic practices, which they extract from their own experiences, histories, identities, and under-standings of rhetorical situations. These various factors open a door to rec-ognizing race, ethnicity, gender, sexual orientation, and class as part of the rhetorical situation because they shape or create code-switching practices.

Moreover, along with Gilyard, they invite scholars to consider the entire rhetorical situation—immediate and larger—for people who code-switch because they function as active agents in reading their rhetorical situation and choosing to perform in specific ways. Above all, these scholars pro-mote an activist and ethical agenda for code switching by advancing better understanding and treatment of Latinxs—that is, there is a commitment to code switching from Licona and an awareness of a wide-ranging audi-ence from Anzaldúa. In other words, these women write and speak in ways that conceptualize a code-switching that promotes inclusivity of the Latinx experiences and practices.

Together, the work these scholars bring to the conversation on code switching offers a decolonial perspective to its conceptualization and practice. Gilyard identifies a colonial force in the study of this practice and challenges current pedagogical implications. Guerra claims bilingual Latinxs employ code-switching practices even when not mixing languages; it's a practice they actively perform at all times. Licona and Anzaldúa infuse their histories, identities, and lived experiences when considering code-switching practices. Their visions and thinking make clear that it entails much more than mixing languages or dialects. Although not exhaustive, here is a definition that arises out of these scholars' writings:

In the context of Spanish and English literacies, code-switching means to read and write codes embedded in colonialist situations that disenfran-chise people because of language, race, ethnicity, class, sexual orientation, and gender. It also acknowledges these colonial situations and commits itself to understanding and sharing the experiences of bilingual Latinxs.

For bilingual Latinxs, it's not enough to navigate two languages (sepa-rate or mixed); these writers also require critical literacy skills that will make them consider colonial practices and forces. This conception of code switching is not meant to overtake the traditional approach—it's sup-posed to enhance it. This expanded definition acknowledges the work that bilingual students already put forth when navigating educational systems, but it also challenges them to develop their bilingual critical literacy skills. It's intended to be a practical approach rather than an idealistic one. The real-world component stems from acknowledging that this definition does not apply to every institution or student. The idealism lies in the belief that the concept of code switching I have described is possible and that students and educators still find usefulness in maintaining or developing bilingual critical literacy skills to enhance their everyday lives.

WORKS CITED

Anzaldúa, Gloria. *Borderlands/La Frontera: The New Mestiza*. San Francisco: Aunt Lute, 1987. Print.

Artze-Vega, Isis, Elizabeth I. Doud, and Belkys Torres. *Más allá del inglés:* A Bilingual Approach to College Composition. In *Teaching Writing with Latino/a Students: Lessons Learned at Hispanic-Serving Institutions*, eds. Cristina Kirklighter, Diana Cárdenas, and Susan Wolff Murphy, 99–117. Albany: State U of New York P, 2007. Print.

Gilyard, Keith. Rethinking the Code-Switching Paradigm. *True to the Language Game: African American Discourse, Cultural Politics, and Pedagogy*, 147–160. New York: Routledge, 2011. Print.

Guerra, Juan C. From Code-Segregation to Code-Switching to Code-Meshing: Finding Deliverance from Deficit Thinking through Language Awareness and Performance. In *61st Yearbook of the Literacy Research Association*, eds. Pamela J. Dunston, Susan King Fullerton, C. C. Bates, Kathy Headley, and Pamela M. Stecker, 29–39. Oak Creek: Literacy Research Association, 2012. Print.

Hall Kells, Michelle. Understanding the Rhetorical Value of *Tejano* Codeswitching. *Latino/a Discourses: On Language, Identity & Literacy Education*, ed. Michelle Hall Kells, Valerie Balester, and Victor Villanueva, 24–39. Portsmouth: Boynton/Cook, 2004. Print.

Hinojosa, Rolando. This Writer's Sense of Place. *A Voice of My Own: Essays and Stories*, 9–16. Houston: Arte Público P, 2011. Print.

Licona, Adela C. *Zines in Third Space: Radical Cooperation and Borderlands Rhetoric*. Albany: State U of New York P, 2012. Print.

Lippi-Green, Rosina. *English with an Accent: Language, Ideology, and Discrimination in the United States*. 2nd ed. New York: Routledge, 2012. Print.

Lunsford, Andrea. Toward a Mestiza Rhetoric: Gloria Anzaldúa on Composition and Postcoloniality. *JAC* 18, no. 1 (1998): 1–27. *JSTOR*. Web. November 3, 2014.

Mejía, Jaime Armin. Arts of the U.S.—Mexico Contact Zone. In *Crossing Borderlands: Composition and Postcolonial Studies*, eds. Andrea A. Lunsford and Lahoucine Ouzgane. Pittsburgh: U of Pittsburgh P, 2004. Print.

Pérez, Emma. *The Decolonial Imaginary: Writing Chicanas into History.* Bloomington: Indiana UP, 1999. Print.

Pew Hispanic Center/Kaiser Family Foundation. *Bilingualism.* Washington, DC: Pew Research Center, 2004. Web. January 19, 2015. www.pewresearch.org

Sánchez, Rosaura. *Chicano Discourse: Socio-historic Perspectives.* Houston: Arte Público P, 1994. Print.

Taylor, Paul, Mark Hugo Lopez, Jessica Martínez, and Gabriel Velasco. *When Labels Don't Fit: Hispanics and Their Views of Identity.* Washington, DC: Pew Research Center, 2012. Web. January 20, 2015. <www.pewresearch.org>

Toribio, Almeida Jacqueline. Spanish-English Code-Switching Among US Latinos. *International Journal of the Sociology of Language* 158, no. 1 (2002): 89–119. *EBSCOHOST.* Web. November 4, 2014.

Valdés Fallis, Guadalupe. Code-Switching in Bilingual Chicano Poetry. *Hispania* 59, no. 4 (1976): 877–886. *JSTOR.* Web. November 3, 2014.

Villa, Daniel. *No nos dejaremos:* Writing in Spanish as an Act of Resistance. In *Latino/a Discourses: On Language, Identity & Literacy Education,* ed. Michelle Hall Kells, Valerie Balester, and Victor Villanueva, 85–95. Portsmouth: Boynton/Cook, 2004. Print.

CHAPTER 6

Writing

Raúl Sánchez

On the one hand, it is easy and common to mystify writing. Theorists, scholars, researchers, and writers in the Western tradition have been doing it for more than 2000 years. They have especially mystified that tradition's preferred mode of writing, alphabetic, endowing it with extraordinary semantic, rhetorical, and intellectual power—and sometimes, as in the case of Plato, danger. From the perspective of modernity and beyond, they have found in this power a key to that tradition's economic and cultural dominance over a large part of the world for the last 500 or so years. To readers of this chapter, perhaps the most familiar example, although in no way the most egregious, will be Walter Ong's claim that "no other writing system restructures the human lifeworld so drastically as alphabetic writing. Or so democratically, for the alphabet is relatively easy to learn" (35).

On the other hand, writing is fairly mysterious, though perhaps differently so than the alphabet's champions suppose. I refer not only to the origins of various writing systems in various cultures or to the theoretical complexities involved in identifying writing as a technology, although these are certainly important issues. Rather, I mean the processes and functions of writing, the act and product itself—mediated and inflected, of course,

R. Sánchez (✉)
Department of English, University of Florida, Gainesville, FL, USA

© The Editor(s) (if applicable) and The Author(s) 2016
I.D. Ruiz, R. Sánchez (eds.), *Decolonizing Rhetoric and Composition Studies*, DOI 10.1057/978-1-137-52724-0_6

by the histories and politics that inform any given writing technology in any given moment and geopolitical location. Contrary to common sense, writing does not simply record or commemorate. As both an event and an object in the world, writing actively participates in the world, and the details of that participation are not easy to decipher.

One important step on the way to figuring out how writing works is to liberate its study from the theoretical and historical provincialism that has dominated it and that we have only recently begun to recognize. I mean, of course, the provincialism that treats Western/European perspectives on knowledge, culture, and language as universal—that is, as not being perspectives at all. This provincialism places unnecessary constraints on what can be thought, understood, observed, and taught as writing in the first place. Implicitly and explicitly, it discounts the achievements, even the humanity, of those who come from cultures with writing traditions different from those of the West.

In the Americas, where Western and Indigenous perspectives on writing and communication have been clashing but also intertwining and, in a sense, reproducing for more than 500 years, the prospect of sorting them out seems conceptually and empirically daunting. But it is possible and necessary, not in order to restore past practices but to better understand contemporary ones. As long as our equipment for understanding, studying, and teaching writing remains provincially Western, it will be inadequate to the task of dealing with contemporary writing practices, which necessarily draw from deep wells of culture and cultural practice—wells unbeknownst even to many of those who do the practicing.

WRITING AS SUCH

In her introduction to the landmark 1994 collection of essays, *Writing Without Words: Alternative Literacies in Mesoamerica and the Andes*, Elizabeth Hill Boone suggests that the study of communication in pre-Conquest America leads to the awareness that scholars must "reach a broader definition of writing" (4). She notes that "in most people's minds," writing is "graphically recorded language." Consequently, from this perspective, "the most advanced writing systems convey speech the most exactly and clearly" (6). For Boone and others, this view, and the corresponding notion that pictorial writing systems reflect a cultural deficiency of some kind, reflects "a European/Mediterranean bias" that must be countered by a view that would "allow all notational systems to be encompassed" regardless of their relationship to speech (9). Without this expanded view, the relationship between Indigenous Américan writing and Western alphabetic writing remains uneven, resulting in a variety of negative consequences, not the least of which is the lack of an objective perspective on writing as such.

And in fact, the two decades since the publication of *Writing Without Words* have produced many studies that examine one or more of the notation systems that predate modern Europeans' arrival in this hemisphere. These studies account for those systems in ways that accord them a status equal to that of alphabetic writing. They examine the systems in themselves as well as their contacts and conflicts with alphabetic writing. But they have been carried out by anthropologists, art historians, and linguists more so than by researchers in the field variably known as composition and rhetoric, composition studies, or writing studies.

Fortunately, this situation changed somewhat in 2008 with the appearance of Damián Baca's *Mestiz@ Scripts, Digital Migrations, and the Territories of Writing*, and then again in 2010 with *Rhetorics of the Americas: 3114 BCE to 2012 CE* by Baca and Victor Villanueva. Together, these books began to bridge the gap between the theoretical and empirical knowledge emerging from the ongoing study of Latin American writing systems and the traditional knowledge bases of contemporary writing studies. Some of these knowledge bases had already been prepared to receive this new work thanks to composition scholars who for some time had drawn on Chicanx and mestiz@ theorists such as Gloria Anzaldúa and Cherríe Moraga. Their work examined—and continues to examine—contemporary discursive practices that are rooted, explicitly and implicitly, in various aspects of indigeneity, *mestizaje*, or both.

Thanks to this work in non-Western rhetorics and literacies, composition studies subject now has at its disposal a theoretically and empirically expansive concept of writing—one that sees as provincial so many of the concepts and assumptions about writing that previously had been considered universal. This is not to say that the work of provincializing the falsely universal, and of identifying uniquely Américan contributions to an actually global conception of writing, is finished. In fact, what the field really has at its disposal now is a new problematic, a potentially better conceptual framework within which to think theoretically, empirically, and pedagogically about writing. And we certainly need such a framework, one that not only incorporates Américan and Latinx forms and modes of inscription but also is profoundly transformed by them.

The most familiar argument in favor of such transforming has to do with demographics, particularly in the United States. As the number of Latin American immigrants and Latinx descendants of immigrants grow, they put increasing pressure on educational, political, and cultural institutions to reflect their varied backgrounds, cultures, and experiences. This process has been underway for decades, particularly in border states and other points of entry (e.g., Florida and New York). But more recently it has become more visible.

More generally, such a framework's potential lies in its ability to help establish a genuinely comparative approach to the study of writing and writing systems rather than an implicitly or explicitly hierarchical perspective. Following such an approach, we would not assume a theory to be universally applicable simply because it is a theory. On the other hand, neither would we assume that its provinciality—that is, the fact that it emerges from a particular locus of enunciation—renders it useless for contemplation across contexts. So, for example, to take seriously Jacques Derrida's theoretical discourse on writing—as Boone, Walter Mignolo, and other Latin Americanists do—is to read it simultaneously on its own terms and on terms we determine to be our own. Moreover, in the particular case of Derrida, such a reading allows us to witness Western Modernity at the outer limits of what that system can imagine about the act of making marks for the purpose of communication.

At those outer limits, perspectives traditional to Western epistemology falter. Specifically, an ingrained tendency breaks down: the habit of looking through writing to that which writing is supposed to represent. Of course, writing (Western or otherwise) does represent; but Western Modernity has had some difficulty imagining other, perhaps more fundamental, functions of writing. Nearly five decades after the initial publication of Derrida's early, radical work—*De la grammatologie* and *L'écriture et la différance* debuted in 1967—we have seen little new theoretical movement in this direction. (One exception might be Gregory Ulmer's work, which is effectively a longitudinal theoretical study of grammatology's pedagogical implications in the context of rapid Western technological change.)

But now, the idea of an Américan writing—of writing conceived on this hemisphere's terms, according to systems and practices developed in these loci of enunciation—suggests the possibility of breaking theoretical ground hand-in-hand with Derrida's critique-from-within. Despite the fact that Mignolo situates Derrida's discourse within the very modernity/coloniality that Mignolo wishes to disrupt, and despite the fact that some scholars criticize Mignolo for—in their view—failing to understand the meaning and to grasp the implications of Derrida's theory of writing, I believe that Derrida's "deconstruction" and Mignolo's "decoloniality" can work together toward what might honestly be called a global and comparative theory of writing. What follows is a first attempt at making this case.

MIGNOLO ON DECOLONIALITY

Of course, I am not a Latin Americanist. I do not have a thorough knowledge of the long-standing and ongoing debates and discussions in that field. Instead, I encounter them at various removes, sometimes in passing, while exploring particular sources regarding certain interesting or relevant issues that deal with my scholarly concerns, or by scouring Works Cited pages and reading as attentively as possible. So when addressing Mignolo's work, even work that deals directly with writing, I acknowledge that I do so as a disciplinary outsider. As such, however, I enjoy the advantage of having no investment in that field's particular pieties. Instead, as a student of composition and rhetoric, I value work in Latin American studies and in other fields exactly insofar as they help me theorize writing. On the other hand, while I like to think that this perspective or attitude gives me a certain amount of freedom, I also know the value of context, so I will try to provide some.

Mignolo's is a major theoretical voice in Latin American studies. Across several books, articles, and essays, he has built on the work of predecessors such as Enrique Dussel, Anibal Quijano, and many others to argue for the development of a distinctly Latin American epistemological space in which to generate and analyze Latin American thought, culture, and history. His terms change as his thinking evolves, but the goal of the project remains more or less the same: to identify the extent (and the limits) of modern European influence on every aspect of Latin American culture, and then to set the conditions by which a specifically Latin American epistemology can be articulated. Such an epistemology necessarily would be multivalent: comprised of Indigenous, African, Asian, and European contributions understood in their fullest possible complexities and taking into account the effects of their complex interactions. As such, it would differ from the prevailing epistemology—that of Western Modernity, whose nearly global reach remains rooted in the places and times of its emergence onto the world scene.

In this context (which, following the historian Dipesh Chakrabarty, we might refer to as *provincializing Europe*) Mignolo replaces the familiar idea of decolonization with the concept of decoloniality. According to Mignolo, decolonization "describes a period and refers to a complex scenario of struggles that today have become an object of study for historians, political scientists, economists, and international law scholars." Historically, its goals were "to expel the imperial administration from the territory, in order for the elites to govern themselves" (*Darker* 53).

In contrast, decoloniality speaks to a condition of "imperialism without colonies" in which a country (or a continent) has achieved political independence but continues to draw its resources of knowledge from the former colonizer or from the larger and enduring "colonial matrix of power" (*Darker* 54). This matrix comprises the ongoing (and thoroughgoing) system of epistemological, ideological, economic, and cultural hegemony that was established, developed, and maintained through European expansion across the globe. It began with Spain and Portugal in the sixteenth century, continued with Great Britain, France, Germany, and lesser European powers in the eighteenth and nineteenth centuries, and culminated with the United States (seen as an extension of Anglo-European power) in the twentieth century. Decoloniality names the process by which we identify "the crooked rhetoric that naturalizes 'modernity' as a universal global process and point of arrival" as well as that rhetoric's "darker side"—the coloniality by which people and areas formerly under colonialism continue to be subordinated epistemologically ("Delinking" 450).

For Mignolo and others, Latin American thought has remained within the epistemological orbit of Western Modernity. This is perhaps ironic because, as Dussel argues in *The Invention of the Americas*, modernity emerged precisely as a result of Europe's encounter with the people and resources of this hemisphere. Mignolo shares this position but extends its consequences. Adapting Gloria Anzaldúa's metaphor of the border, he searches for ways to imagine not an absolute exteriority to this nearly all-encompassing world system but rather the double consciousness that necessarily inhabits the boundaries and overlays where systems meet and effectively create different, new systems.

According to Linda Martín Alcoff, Mignolo's particular concept of border thinking is intended "to specify the locality of subaltern knowledge as a border location rather than simply the beyond of Western knowledge or the site of pure difference" (93). The idea is not to retrieve a purely precolonial epistemology, but rather to recognize how the heretofore hidden, unnatural quality of Western epistemology had been presented as, simply, epistemology. Of course, one way to gain such perspective would be to study the modes and forms of thinking and writing that precede the period of conquest—again, not to restore or reclaim their past glory as such but to place them on equal analytical footing with Western modes and forms and to reveal the provintiality of those Western modes and forms. This explains Mignolo's early interest in Américan writing and his extended engagement with Derrida's work on writing.

MIGNOLO ON DECONSTRUCTION

Mignolo appropriately situates Derrida's work within Western Modernity. He acknowledges the formidable challenge Derrida poses to that tradition, but he also sees it as being fundamentally of that tradition. Thus, for Mignolo, Derrida's approach to writing cannot by itself prompt the profound reorientation—the gesture toward decoloniality—that Mignolo seeks. Derrida's critique might push Western Modernity toward Western postmodernity (i.e., toward its own limits), but as Mignolo sees it, such a shift takes place within the same epistemological framework.

This is not to say that Mignolo finds no relevance in Derrida's work. In the afterword to *Writing Without Words*, he takes up the task of "rereading Derrida's grammatology from the experience of the Americas" (302–303). This means, first, acknowledging that Derrida's argument proceeds from a particular "locus of enunciation." It means marking the limits and limitations of that locus, revealing as provincial what had been considered universal. And it means identifying "alternative loci of enunciation" that provide an epistemological fresh start to the study of writing and culture, preparing the ground for genuinely comparative analyses rather than the evaluative and hierarchical approaches that characterize Western Modernity's encounters with other forms of communication during its domination of the world scene ("Afterword" 303).

Toward this end, Mignolo situates Derrida's interest in writing "in the intellectual debate of the sixties, as well as [Derrida's] political intervention in France," and he argues that this situation "cannot be projected toward" pre-Conquest Américan writing "without risking an academic colonialism."

Derrida's critique of Western notions of writing is "devastating" but "not automatically relevant" to a discussion of writing systems that precede the arrival of Europeans, nor to the subsequent period of "coexistence and transformation" between these systems and that of the Europeans ("Afterword" 303). Moreover, Mignolo notes Derrida's recognition of his own tradition's limitations, pointing to Derrida's need to "invent the notion of 'difference'" in order to break free of the view of writing as representation of speech ("Afterword" 304).

But, from Mignolo's perspective, that which Derrida has to invent from within Western Modernity is already available in other places. From a locus of enunciation informed by Mesoamerican and Andean writing systems, it is possible to arrive at "a different notion of writing that allows for a rethinking of the relationship between speech and writing" ("Afterword" 305). This locus allows one to recognize a variety of human modes of inscription, for a variety of purposes, using a variety of materials. Within this increased variety, "the interrelations of visible signs with sounds to coordinate behaviors is certainly diverse," but it is not limited to the capture of speech ("Afterword" 306). In fact, seen in this context, the Western focus on alphabetic writing seems rather anomalous and, again, provincial. As Mignolo notes, "how it happened, then, that in the history of humanity a set of visible signs closely connected with sounds has been achieved, and why it became so pervasive in a region of the globe north of the Mediterranean Sea which extended itself over the Atlantic, is a story that has not yet been told in any detail" ("Afterword" 306–307). Of course, what we might characterize as "anomalous" is precisely what previous scholars (and apologists) of modernity would call "exceptional." In other words, the old idea that alphabetic writing is uniquely good at developing, recording, and distributing complex ideas is precisely what books such as *Writing Without Words* have sought to dispel.

At any rate, Derrida's theoretical analysis of this particular kind of writing does offer one way to recognize its heretofore hidden provinciality, and this is what Mignolo sees as its contribution to the decentering and de-universalizing of Western epistemology and modernity, as well as to the "dismantling [of] an ideology of writing working in complicity with imperial expansion and with postcolonial nation building." In this sense, Mignolo sees Derrida's critique from within Western Modernity and recent reappraisals of Andean and Mesoamerican writing systems— which had been "left off the map" of "canonical histories of writing"—as working toward similar (though not identical) ends from very different locations ("Afterword" 307).

MIGNOLO "DECONSTRUCTED"

But although Mignolo appreciates Derrida's analysis of Western writing, he does not believe the same analysis necessarily applies to other writing systems. Here Mignolo's position hinges on the idea that what is being "deconstructed" is the particular relationship between speech and writing that is unique to alphabetic writing. Scott Michaelsen and Scott Cutler Shershow take issue with this idea, and in the process they call into question Mignolo's entire project. They start by noting that Mignolo fails to fully enlist Derrida in his cause, noting that the latter's "critique of a logocentrism that is first and last also an ethnocentrism" could have been applied to the colonial imposition of alphabetic writing on indigenous people (40). Instead, they argue, Mignolo does the opposite: he casts Derrida as part of the problem his project is trying to overcome; he believes Derrida is "'blind' to the radical epistemological and ontological otherness" of colonial subjects and that this blindness opens the door to epistemological colonialism—the condition of coloniality (40).

Michaelsen and Shershow note that while Mignolo elaborates this argument over several texts and in several ways, it is based on the core claim "that Amerindian systems of signification were so distinctively different as to escape the problems Derrida described under the term 'logocentrism'" (43). The problem with this claim, as they see it, is that Mignolo wants to have it both ways: he wants to claim that pre-Columbian writing systems are as sophisticated as alphabetic writing, but he wants to deny that they are subject to the same theoretical problems as alphabetic writing—problems that Derrida's analyses painstakingly point out.

It is worth noting, again, the considerable amount of work that has gone precisely into showing that pre-Columbian sign systems are in fact forms of writing, that they should be understood and studied as writing, and that they thereby expand the very idea of writing. We are well past the point at which that argument needs to be made. In fact, Michaelsen and Shershow point to Boone's own enlistment of Derrida "as an ally in reclaiming the pictographic systems of pre-Columbian as legitimate forms of 'writing'" (44). They cite her claim that these systems allowed for "accountability, memory, and interpretability" (45).

They note that despite being entirely or partly nonphonetic, this writing is nevertheless "linked to some semiotic 'message' or 'content' that both precedes and survives its inscription, that is reproducible as 'voice' or 'reading' in its wake, and that thus anchors or limits the varied readings or voicing of the inscribed signs" (45). Therefore, according to Michaelsen and Shershow, despite its different relationship to speech, it works just like alphabetic writing.

From this critique of Mignolo's basic claim about writing, Michaelsen and Shershow go on to question the entirety of Mignolo's project. And it is here that they misstep and overreach. For while Mignolo may indeed overstate differences between the various pre-Columbian writing systems and European/alphabetic writing (particularly on the matter of Derrida's notion of *différance*), it does not follow that the entire project of identifying a separate epistemological, hermeneutic, or enunciative space particular to Latin America necessarily falls apart. In fact, even if Mignolo himself were to agree that his project hinged on the radical distinction he proposes between the writing systems, he would be mistaken.

For Michaelsen and Shershow, at stake is the question of exteriority—the ability to imagine and inhabit space beyond Western Modernity's epistemological and ideological influence. Mignolo's border thinking does require at least a notion of epistemological exteriority—a border separates two spaces, after all, however artificially—and from a certain postmodern perspective this is indeed very problematic. Nonetheless, pointing to metaphysics (in the Derridean sense of that term) informing Mignolo's position is simply not enough, theoretically speaking. In such a mode of critique, one is merely debunking an argument by pointing to the quicksand on which it—like every other argument—ultimately stands. Instead, we might go beyond critique and ask what Mignolo wants to achieve by taking on the border metaphor and its invocation of radical exteriority.

There may be several reasons, but the most important one, from my own disciplinary perspective, is to shift the discussion away from the philosophical and toward the rhetorical, the cultural, and the political—terrain that happens to be more amenable, familiar, and relevant to composition studies. So although Mignolo's project comes under harsh criticism by Michaelsen and Shershow, as well as others, such criticisms are not entirely relevant to the task at hand, which ultimately is not philosophical. In fact, and despite Mignolo's own terminology, the task at hand is not even epistemological.

It is rhetorical. Mignolo's decoloniality is of interest to scholars in our field who wish to continue expanding the concept of writing, especially as we continue to consider the rich varieties of Latin American and Latinx written experience past, present, and future. Regardless of decoloniality's ultimate fate in the discourse of philosophy or critical theory, a copious and useful theory of writing requires decoloniality as its conceptual horizon. As I have noted elsewhere, the very idea of writing already suggests such a horizon (Sánchez 244). Mignolo's theory of decoloniality offers a vocabulary for naming it in greater detail.

MARK-MAKING, OR ALL LIVING THINGS ARE WRITERS

Although my interest in Mignolo's work is rhetorical rather than philosophical, I hasten to note that my commitment to and interest in rhetoric has its limits. In composition studies, it is customary to treat rhetoric as a descriptive, even generic term for something like *purposeful language use*. There is also the field's long-standing habit of invoking and studying rhetorical theory, the rhetorical tradition, the history of rhetoric, and even histories of rhetorics, by which we usually mean some version or feature of the familiar 2000-year-old narrative that begins in the northern Mediterranean. I am happy to witness the ongoing decentering and denaturalizing of the authors, texts, concepts, and practices associated with that narrative, and I do not take as given its relevance to the study of writing. For me, rhetoric—especially the activity known as rhetorical theory—is interesting only to the extent that it can shed light on writing, and that extent is limited.

It is limited because writing and rhetoric seem equally metaphorical, though in somewhat different ways. Certainly, both are encumbered with histories that compromise their ability to describe things or events in the world. In particular, rhetoric seems so tethered to Western epistemology—including but of course not limited to Western Modernity—that I doubt its ability to be descriptive. Description, in the form of the genuinely comparative approach alluded to earlier, is precisely what is needed if we want to theorize, study, and teach mark-making in a broader-than-merely alphabetic sense—that is, mark-making at the borders between Western Modernity and the Indigenous cultures of this hemisphere.

As I mentioned previously, the very notion of writing calls forth its own conceptual horizon, by which I mean its own conditions of possibility and impossibility. This is basically Derrida's argument about writing as laid out in *Of Grammatology*, "Signature Event Context," and elsewhere. It is an argument that depends on a simultaneously broad and precise definition of writing, and one that has at least glimpsed the West's provincialism. Somewhat snarkily, Ong asks: "When does a footprint or a deposit of faeces or urine (used by many species of animals for communication) become writing?" He then claims that to identify as writing "any semiotic marking" is to trivialize writing as such, to ignore the "critical and unique breakthrough into new kinds of noetic operations and new worlds of knowledge" that the invention of writing made possible. But, of course, Ong is referring here to alphabetic writing, to "a coded system of visible marks...whereby a writer could determine, in effect without limit, the exact words and sequence of words that a reader would generate from a given text" (34). So Ong's concern about writing's trivialization has a limit. In turn, this suggests that although his theoretical insights into alphabetic writing may be profound, they do not necessarily tell us something about writing as such.

In fact, we might ask: why *shouldn't* we consider footprints or other semiotic marks to be writing? If we agree with Kenneth Burke that "all living things are critics"—if we accept his examples of trout and chickens and humans who read the signs around them—then the thought that they might also write the signs around them is perhaps not so far-fetched (5). Far from trivializing, to see writing as consequential mark-making is to begin the process of delinking it from the ideological, epistemological, and rhetorical baggage that burdens its study. It is a first step toward a time when we might be able to study and understand writing in its fullest complexity.

WORKS CITED

Alcoff, Linda Martín. Mignolo's Epistemology of Coloniality. *CR: The New Centennial Review 7* (2007): 79–101.

Baca, Damián. *Mestiz@ Scripts, Digital Migrations, and the Territories of Writing.* New York: Palgrave, 2008. Print.

Baca, Damián, and Victor Villanueva. *Rhetorics of the Americas: 3114 BCE to 2012 CE.* New York: Palgrave, 2010. Print.

Boone, Elizabeth Hill. Introduction: Writing and Recording Knowledge. Boone and Mignolo, 3–26. Print.

Boone, Elizabeth Hill, and Walter D. Mignolo, eds. *Writing without Words: Alternative Literacies in Mesoamerica and the Andes.* Durham, NC: Duke UP, 1994. Print.

Burke, Kenneth. *Permanence and Change: An Anatomy of Purpose.* 3rd ed. Berkeley: U of California P, 1984 (1935).

Chakrabarty, Dipesh. *Provincializing Europe: Postcolonial Thought and Historical Difference.* Reissue. Princeton: Princeton UP, 2000. Print.

Derrida, Jacques. *De la grammatologie.* Paris: Les Éditions de Minuit, 1967a. Print.

Derrida, Jacques. *L'écriture et la différance.* Paris: Les Éditions de Minuit, 1967b. Print.

Derrida, Jacques. *Of Grammatology,* corrected ed. Trans. Gayatri Chakravorty Spivak. Baltimore: Johns Hopkins UP, 1997.

Derrida, Jacques. Signature Event Context. *Margins of Philosophy.* Trans. Alan Bass. Chicago: U of Chicago P, 1982 (1972).

Dussel, Enrique. *The Invention of the Americas: Eclipse of "the Other" and the Myth of Modernity.* Trans. Michael D. Barber. New York: Continuum, 1995. Print.

Michaelsen, Scott, and Scott Cutler Shershow. Rethinking Border Thinking. *South Atlantic Quarterly* 106 (2007): 39–60. Print.

Mignolo, Walter D. Afterword: Writing and Recorded Knowledge in Colonial and Postcolonial Situations. Boone and Mignolo, 293–313. Print.

Mignolo, Walter D. Delinking: The Rhetoric of Modernity, the Logic of Coloniality, and the Grammar of De-Coloniality. *Cultural Studies* 21 (2007): 449–514. Print.

Mignolo, Walter D. *The Darker Side of Western Modernity: Global Futures, Decolonial Options.* Durham, NC: Duke UP, 2011. Print.

Ong, Walter J. Writing is a Technology that Restructures Thought. In *The Written Word: Literacy in Transition (Wolfson College Lectures, 1985),* ed. Gerd Baumann. Oxford: Clarendon P, 1986.

Sánchez, Raúl. Outside the Text: Retheorizing Empiricism and Identity. *College English* 74 (2012): 234–246.

PART III

Self-(Re)Definitions

CHAPTER 7

Poch@

Cruz Medina

Back in 2011, I first exchanged blog posts with Romeo Guzmán, a Ph.D. history candidate at Columbia University who wrote a blog called *Pocho in Greater Mexico*. This collaboration began in part because of Guzmán's self-identification with the title of this chapter. I have long been fascinated by the poch@ trope, beginning with discussions with the *mexicano* cooks in the San Diego restaurant where I waited tables after a stint teaching third grade in Puntarenas, Costa Rica. This interest continued when my father died and I inherited boxes of his books, which included a tattered 1970 edition of the book *Pocho* (Villarreal). In Spanish, *pocho* means "bruised fruit" (Wilson), but it is better known as a pejorative term for "cultural traitor" (Villareal; Rodriguez; Anzaldúa).

As an educator, I was attracted to the term because I valued its potential as a decolonial trope for Latinx students in the United States. As Marissa M. Juárez explains: "When people use *pocha* as solely a derogatory marker of identity, they become complicit in the systems of domination that have historically served to marginalize and to Other the brown body." But the etymology of *poch@* opens up a decolonial epistemology

C. Medina (✉)
Department of English, Santa Clara University, Santa Clara, CA, USA

© The Editor(s) (if applicable) and The Author(s) 2016
I.D. Ruiz, R. Sánchez (eds.), *Decolonizing Rhetoric and Composition Studies*, DOI 10.1057/978-1-137-52724-0_7

93

that lets us reimagine it as a positive term, even a term of resistance. This is exactly what happens in a series of blog posts by Latinx rhetoric and composition scholars. This chapter examines how a group of academic bloggers repurpose *poch@* and, in the process, reclaim the right to name themselves on their own terms rather than those of the dominant Latinx culture.

My study of blog posts as decolonial sites connects with my previous study of Twitter microblogs that allow Latinx students to build support networks and perform ethnic and linguistic diversity while increasing the clarity of their online messages (Medina). It also shares goals with Ellen Cushman's contribution to the 2013 special issue of *College English*, in which she asks how methods for recontextualizing digital archives can decolonize those technological spaces.

In composition studies, scholars have analyzed certain Latinx texts, such as Richard Rodriguez's1982 *Hunger of Memory*, as literacy narratives and as assimilation rhetoric (Young; Martinez; Villanueva, *Bootstraps*), while others have extended the work of Gloria Anzaldúa's *Borderlands/ La Frontera* (Lunsford; Baca; Licona). Still, little attention has been paid to the *poch@* trope that many within the Latinx community use against their own.

Performance artist Guillermo Gómez-Peña explains how the trope serves as a colonial instrument: "[I]f you crossed the border you *ipso-facto* became a renegade, a traitor, a pocho. That was a complete fallacy based on a very old-fashioned binary model of identity" (208). Previously, I have examined how artists, such as Gómez-Peña, embrace *poch@* as a subversive trope while uncovering the term's pre-Columbian connection to the *pochteca* traveling merchant.[1] Here, I extend my examination into the digital realm by looking at how Latinx composition and rhetoric scholars problematize and embrace the trope, engage with its decolonial potential, and attribute new knowledge-building interpretations in the tradition of Anzaldúa's reclamation of *mestizaje*.

Decolonial Tropes as Serious as a Heart Attack

In certain ways, for Latinxs in composition and rhetoric, the figure of the poch@ speaks also to their subject positions in the field. This might have to do with the fact that the percentage of Latinx faculty is shockingly disproportionate[2] to the percentage of Latinxs in the US population. Although the field publishes scholarship on theory and pedagogy for Latinxs, it has trouble seeing Latinx teachers, researchers, and theorists as full colleagues.

For example, Todd Ruecker's 2014 essay, "Here They Do This, There They Do That: Latinas/ Latinos Writing across Institutions," unknowingly perpetuates a colonialist narrative in which Latinxs are sites of analysis but not scholars whose work might inform the essay's theory, review of literature, or analysis of data, apart from a passing reference to Villanueva's *Bootstraps*. Yet, Latinx scholars produce not only sites of analysis but also tertiary scholarship, as do non-Latinx scholars of color who demonstrate a decolonial ethos in academic research.

Drawing on research from scholars of color performs the decolonial act that Walter Mignolo defines as "delinking," by which he means "to change the terms and not just the content of the conversation," thereby changing the content more profoundly (459). The new terms of this conversation facilitate a discussion about writing, students, and educators that extends beyond the colonial gate-keeping of composition studies. In that field, Geneva Smitherman called attention to the importance of minoritized language and how African American language imbues the colonial English language with meaning meant to resist it. Writing after the Oakland School Board's Resolution on Ebonics, Smitherman responds to the attacks on the legitimacy of the linguistic tradition of African American Language (AAL):

> Slang, after all, is rather lighthearted and harmless, and it's usually short-lived—here today, gone tomorrow—but the social critique embodied in Black slang is SERIOUS AS A HEART ATTACK.... Africans in America flipped the script, making an alien tongue their own by imbuing "ole massa's" language with their unique, African semantics. Words came to have double meanings as their definitions shifted according to the situation and were infused with irony, metaphor, and ambiguity. (3)

Smitherman outlines the rhetorical power of what neocolonial power dismisses as "Black slang" by explaining that the incorporation of this slang and subversive signifiers has led to the improvisation and innovation of key terms.

Victor Villanueva draws attention to the connection between colonialism and race, and he specifically acknowledges the problematic notion of internal colonialism because journal reviewers reject "resurrecting" Franz Fanon ("On the Rhetoric" 655). Decolonial tropes and key terms delink from narratives perpetuated in internal colonialism that appropriates and stigmatizes the rhetorical efficacy of previous self-identifiers. In her discussion of African American self-identification, Smitherman explains: "Name changes and debates over names reflect our uncertain status and come to the forefront during crises and up-heavals in the Black condition" (6). For people of color, decolonial terms, such as *poch@*, demonstrate the struggle to grapple with the internal colonialism imposed by the field and the crises of methodology; pedagogy; and epistemology that result from writing, teaching, and living in an unsettling, colonized, and "settled" world.

DECOLONIAL FRAMEWORKS AND BLOGS AS DIGITAL ARCHIVES

Although blogs as archives could be charged with furthering the imperial work of collecting artifacts of the Other (Powell "Dreaming"), the analysis of blog contributions by Latinx composition and rhetoric scholars demonstrates how digital spaces can provide alternative platforms (Haas) for discursive practices that challenge and complicate colonial standards, traditions, and narratives about writing. Approaching decoloniality from digital media seems in itself contradictory; however, Angela Haas explains that blogs function as decolonial technological interruptions within our academic literacy practices:

> [A]s part of this decolonial methodology and pedagogy ... with students maintaining their own individual blogs so that others in the discipline might read, engage with, and learn from the inquiry of our online learning community ... the class's digital intellectual work would help to inform others in the public sphere about colonial influences on the agency of specific racialized populations in relation to technology, thereby decolonizing our habits of mind and corresponding rhetorics as they pertain to race and technology relations. (297–298)

To delink from colonial epistemology, Haas asserts that composing in digital modes decolonizes the habit with which dominant (neo)colonial rhetoric regards race. Haas's assertion, in fact, parallels my solicitation of

Latinx colleagues to contribute to my blog, specifically prompting them to meditate on the *poch@* trope.

Decolonial theory as methodology for critique and rhetoric of resistance (Casey) provides a useful point of departure for work with *poch@* and blogs because both possess negative connotations in dominant discourses of identity and knowledge-production. Mignolo's call to change the terms and the conversation is particularly salient because these terms are what ultimately substantiate, authorize, and validate the ways of knowing described by them. Delinking from the power structured into the epistemology of Western (neo)coloniality has important implications for how US Latinxs conceptualize themselves as scholars, educators, and makers of knowledge.

To understand that the term *poch@* possesses rhetorical power is a part of "the work of epistemic delinking, which resituates understanding from the decolonial perspectives that emerged as a counterpoint to modern/colonial thought" (Mignolo quoted in Cushman 119). Key terms and tropes occupy the epistemological space that perpetuates the "perverse logic" that maintains the gate-keeping mechanism of language (Mignolo 450), thereby constructing identity according to that logic's myths of authenticity.

By analyzing blog posts, I perform the decolonial method of participatory research that de-centers the traditional imperial power of the interviewer by co-creating knowledge with the archived writing of these Latinx scholars (Smith). The colonial dynamic between interviewer and interviewee places the control of the latter's responses in the hands of the former. To avoid this, the majority of the quotes remain mostly intact. The analysis that follows in the next section is framed around longer block quotes that actively tell stories, propose theoretical interpretations, and think through feelings and memories. Mignolo's notion of delinking, along with Haas's advocacy of blogs as decolonial practice, and Cushman's argument for the decolonial potential of digital archives inform how what is here approaches the decolonial potential of *poch@* in the new media object of a blog.

POCH@S IN ACADEMIA

The contributors to my blog, *Academia de Cruz Medina* by and large complicate and critique the colonial way of thinking imposed by a trope that imposes a standard of ethnic authenticity. Each contributor focuses *poch@*, and the posts demonstrate the diversity of Latinx identities and experiences. As we see in the examples that follow, the online platform of blogs created something of a third, or interstitial, space (Anzaldúa; Pérez; Licona) outside of traditional academic platforms for communication. Contributors integrate multiple modalities ranging from family reunion photos and home videos to third-party images, as well as traditional academic citations.

In a post titled "Inclusiveness, Exclusivity and Mistaken Identity," Andy Besa recounts how Anglos often frame him as the subject of colonial fetishisms, compelled to taxonomize him as "Other." As a Latinx in Texas, or *tejano*, Besa writes that Anglos exclude and romanticize him as a Native Other. Conversely, in his experiences with non-Whites, he is identified inclusively. Besa notes:

> These references ... offer a glimpse into the minds of those who wish to define and assign identities to those who do not resemble them.... I've experienced this on several times, most often being mistaken for a Native American (technically true) or a Polynesian. The "Are you a Native American?" question always comes from Anglos, while the Polynesian questions have come from other Polynesians (Fijians and Hawaiians). The Anglos' questions always seem to be about *pigeon-holing*, separating me from them and assigning me to a group; they want to determine my identity, assign me membership in a group, and move along.

Besa's experiences as a *poch@* directly reflect "the imperial archive's penchant for collecting, classifying, and isolating," and the decolonial impetus that motivates Mignolo's notion of delinking (Cushman 116). The motivation to redefine terms to change the content that Mignolo describes comes from the "pigeon-holing" that Besa experiences as a person of color whose identity is ascribed a narrative based on the colonial system of labeling.

The difference between labeling and self-identifying highlights the fact that tropes are rhetorical, and Besa channels the rhetorical aspect of self-identifying, imbuing it with a subversive message. Besa notes that he responds to the seemingly complimentary question about his possible Native American identity from Anglos with satire, responding subversively:

> No. Well, yes, I just don't know my tribe. I'm a man without a people (I say it sadly). Most likely, we are northern Coahuiltecans, my family has been in

the Eagle Pass/Piedras Negras area for at least a couple of hundred years...
my native ancestors made the conscious decision to leave their native identities behind, possibly because the waves of biological warfare had utterly
destroyed their cohesiveness as a tribe.... I go for guilt, and choose to point
out that the source of the natives' deaths is in fact, European intrusion.

Besa's satire is not without truth: the Coahuiltecan people was a collective name for small autonomous bands of Native Americans in Northern
Mexico and Southern Texas, from where Besa originated, and they mixed
with Latinxs in the area, which is the *mestizaje* of the borderlands about
which Anzaldúa theorizes (Newcomb).

Besa's response, however, moves beyond the imperial binary of the
Anglo question-poser, provoking a dialogue in which the narrative is
reclaimed and put back on the questioner. This kind of irreverent, trick-
ster response is a decolonial strategy that Kelly describes as détournement,
which turns criticism on the question-poser, revealing the embedded racism in the essentialism, or at the very least fetishism of the native Other
(170).

Although Besa comments critically on the perception from outside the
Latinx community, Aja Y. Martinez points out the necessity to decolonize the internal narratives such as those that resist education. In "Three
Generations *Pocha*," Martinez reconciles the linguistic aspect of her ethnic
identity that *poch@* signifies in the texts of Richard Rodriguez and Gloria
Anzaldúa. Martinez recognizes how oversimplistic the term can be when
it implies "lacking ethnic authenticity" after she learns that her grandfa-
ther was also called *poch@*:

> I felt like I was maybe the first generation to embody "pocho" qualities such
> as my lack of Spanish-speaking skills and a way of presenting myself that got
> me accused of "trying to be white" by some Chicanos I attended school
> with. So to hear my grandpa say that he too faced these accusations I began
> to really wonder about this word and what it means. Does "pocho" mean
> acting white? Does it refer to those of us affected by American ideology and
> values? One American value I subscribe to is education, and it seems the
> further I go in academia the whiter I become to Chicanos from my family
> and 'hood I grew up in. (Martinez)

In working out what it means to be *poch@*, Martinez identifies the implicit
assumption that becoming educated equates to "trying to be white" by

some members of her Chican@ community. This conflation unfortunately has been espoused by Rodriguez's assimilation rhetoric.

Rodriguez identifies *poch@* as indicative of successful assimilation: "*Pocho* then they called me...naming the Mexican-American who, in becoming an American, forgets his native society" (29). Although conservative opponents of bilingual education have championed *Hunger of Memory*, the subtext of the autobiography is about the loss of intimacy that Rodriguez feels for his family and community (Velasco). Martinez rejects Rodriguez's uncritical acceptance of assimilation because she recognizes the larger ideological project of colonization that promotes either/or binaries to separate community ties, as in the case of Rodriguez.

Referencing the films *Mi Familia* and *Barbershop*, Martinez identifies and resists how the educated person of color is portrayed as cultural traitor, a narrative that proliferates through stereotypical media representations. Martinez explains that "I don't like the equation these films promote which goes something like this: ethnic + education = sellout wannabe white, and in our case the 'pocho.' I've been called a 'pocho' in this sense, because to some of my family the more educated I become the more white I am" (Martinez).

Embedded in this cinematic trope of the "wannabe white" character is the narrative cliché of the educated person learning some kind of magical aspect of ethnic authenticity from less educated characters; this stereotypical plot point insidiously reinforces colonial rhetoric against people of color becoming educated. Moreover, the magical quality of authenticity evokes Paulo Freire's description of the oppressed viewing themselves within the oppressor's narrative and least capable of reading the world and naming the oppressor (Freire 17). To ignore oppressive narratives allows the colonizers to mystify the world by naming it as they wish the colonized to read and interpret it.

In her blog post, "A Chicana Feminist Reflection on what it Means to be Pocha," Marissa M. Juárez further untangles the complexity of *poch@* self-identification. She traces her coming into a Chicana feminist consciousness by reflecting on her undergraduate reading of José Antonio Villareal's *Pocho*. Juárez explains her sense of discomfort with narrowly reading *Pocho* as a story highlighting the negative aspects of assimilation:

Richard Rubio, to many in the class, *era un vendido*—a punk-ass-sell-out who was too cowardly and ignorant to assert any pride in his Mexican heritage. I remember feeling embarrassed because I understood and empathized with Richard's plight to find his identity between conflicting Mexican and American values. I kept silent, afraid that if I gave voice to this empathy, my classmates might find out my secret, might see me as less of a Chicana because of it. (Juárez)

Anzaldúa's a new mestiza consciousness submits that the contradictions, which Juárez discusses, are representative of a bicultural, borderlands experience. Juárez also prefaces her reflection on *Pocho* with a quote from Cherríe Moraga that acknowledges the complexity of her experience: "I am a woman with a foot in both worlds; and I refuse the split. I feel the necessity for dialogue" (34).

Focusing on embodiment and the performative nature of identity, Juárez critiques how bodies come to be signified by those who inaccurately construct the identity of an Other. She explains:

I know what it's like to feel like my brown body is being read and signified by people who have no idea what it means to live in a brown body… *both* my brown body *and* my experiences within multiple locations (Mexican, Anglo, and in between) have shaped who I am: A person some might call *pocha*. But one does not have to give up one culture in order to enter another.… From a Chicana feminist perspective, *pocha* might be better understood as one instantiation of *mestizaje*.

Juárez recognizes the rhetorical quality of *poch@* that follows the way Anzaldúa reclaims the notion and term *mestizaje*, despite prior negative connotations. In doing so, she also highlights the rhetorical quality of *poch@* that performs various identities in different contexts. This point echoes what Stuart Hall explains in an interview: "[I]dentity is always in the making…there is no final, finished identity position or self simply then to be produced by the writing" (Drew 207–208).

Inspired by Marissa M. Juárez's post, Natalie A. Martínez further builds on Chicana feminist embodiment, but through a queer approach. In "Poch@ as Queer Racial Melancholia," Martínez grapples with "poch@ as a potential structure of feeling that is a product" of colonial legacies mediated through private spaces (Natalie Martínez). Comparing *poch@* to Gabriela Sandoval's use of Coatlicue, Martínez explains:

Poch@ shares this similar strand of concern. Largely defined as a Mexican-American who is rejected or assimilated into dominant culture, this rejection has mostly been linked to the language or discourse one uses.... I think conceiving of poch@ as a form of queer racial melancholia and similar lines of inquiry are important and timely.... Largely, the affective (re) turn or (re)valuing of "emotion's rhetoricity" has by and large returned to Greco-Roman traditions in what appears to be a seamless recovery of the body for the discipline's already unchallenged historiography. Doing so whether intentional or not erases the contributions writers, artists, and activists have long understood as an interstitial life: one felt, lived, and experienced in and on the body among other bodies—*because of identities.* (Natalie Martínez)

Martínez focuses on the body and the visibility of its marked difference—the marked, racialized difference that colonial logic records in historical notations and physical archives.

Specifically, Martínez performs Cushman's call to recontextualize texts by discussing a recontextualized family vacation video in the context of scholarly voiceover that enunciates what is unsaid by texts on their own: "to decolonize the archive through historiography that seeks to *re*-place media in the languages, practices, and histories of the communities in which they are created" (Cushman 116). Martínez makes meaning from the archival videos that document her life, although the contextualization of this material by the written and visual images that accompany the video incorporates an ethical social practice that allows Martínez, as archival video subject, to write, speak, and re-present herself.

In "Phenomenology and Etymology of a Fresa," Enrique Reynoso asserts that in the borderlands of the Rio Grande Valley (RGV), *poch@* is less common than the pejorative trope *fresa*, which functions within a colonial paradigm of class, gender, and sexuality. Outlining his methodology, Reynoso explains in his post that he solicited crowd-sourced feedback from friends in the RGV on Facebook in order to interpret numerous perspectives on the term *poch@*. Even though Reynoso regards the tropes as somewhat in opposition to one another—*fresa* as upper-class Mexican American as opposed to the assimilated working-class *poch@*—he concludes that both reinforce a colonial Other-ing:

[F]resa is (an admittedly late) response to *pocho*. *Pocho* lost its teeth because *pochos* have assimilated and are more of a majority than *fresas*. It's a conscious antagonism towards the upper class.... He is from an(O)ther class, not mine. It brings to mind what Kenneth Burke refers to as congregation via segregation—we have to separate the Other in order to create our "own" self. In labeling and transforming the *fresa*, *pocho* has created a monster that nobody wants to claim. *Fresa* is the monster constantly deferred. (Reynoso)

Reynoso criticizes how internal colonialism functions in the RGV because the discourse of people in that space recontextualizes colonial terms in unsettling ways. Reynoso complicates the use of fresa by explaining that "it's also a more subconscious and insidious dig at sexuality. By picking a red, sweet fruit as the embodiment of Mexican masculinity, *pocho* takes a potshot by implying homosexuality" (Reynoso). Reynoso's illustration of heteronormativity enforced through colonial binaries ascribed to *poch@* parallels Anzaldúa's experience of rejection by Chican@s in the RGV: "As a lesbian I have no race, my own people disclaim me" (102). These imperial legacies impose worldviews on the subjugated people, which in turn frame any difference of class, race, gender, sexuality, or disability as a deficit.

CONCLUSION

I return to Romeo Guzmán's post because he cogently summarizes the critical hope possible when studying and practicing decoloniality. Guzmán's *poch@* research in Mexico City provides an important example for creating local archives that document the social epistemic of a time, space, and people, while asking an important question about how we further collaborate and create community:

I am currently involved in helping found a cultural, intellectual, and archival space in Mexico City. Mainly, I'm trying to get as many pocho/a artists, intellectuals, writers, etc. down to Mexico City to engage Mexicans and as many Mexicans up here to engage Chicanos/pochos/etc. ... the most pressing question of our generation: how do we build a politics that reflects our transnational/undocumented/documented communities? (Guzmán)

Although Mignolo's notion of delinking may read as breaking off from all Western systems of thought, the work of Guzmán—like that of Haas and Cushman—demonstrates a practical method for creating alternative spaces for nonhegemonic, archival episteme. Guzmán's desire to create an inclusive archive in Mexico City follows Cushman's explanation that "[s]cholars can begin to decolonize the archive by considering ways in which the archive itself, as well as the materials inside, work within communities" (Cushman 131). *Poch@/Chican@/ Mexican@* archives in Mexico City serve a similar purpose as the blog collaboration that increased communication and built knowledge among contributors outside of traditional conference and publication spaces.

By writing and archiving in digital spaces, such as blogs, these Latinx composition and rhetoric scholars, writers, and teachers have made public their discussions about bodies, identity, and conflict, which are often de-authorized as private. Incorporating a term from Spanish into writing in English does not, on its own, delink from Western literacy and epistemology. After all, Spanish is yet another colonial language that replaced the dominant Nahuatl language of the indigenous Aztec people, who spread their own form of colonialism throughout what is now northern and central Mexico (Mejía). The fact that people, histories, and language cannot escape colonial legacies provides motivation for changing the terms of the conversation and breaking from colonial narratives and topoi.

Cushman acknowledges that delinking from the primacy of English is an ongoing process, and the blog posts, like the essays in this book, begin from the decolonial impulse to resist, survive, and subvert rhetorical narratives of (neo)colonialism that blame the victims of imperial greed. We submit these terms, like new words on the street, giving a name to what we cannot say in front of those who will not let us say it.

NOTES

1. See my *Reclaiming Poch@ Pop: Examining the Rhetoric of Cultural Deficiency.*
2. In "On the Rhetoric of Racism," Victor Villanueva (1999) cites the statistic as less than one percent in English Studies.

WORKS CITED

Anzaldúa, Gloria. *Borderlands: The New Mestiza/La Frontera.* San Francisco: Spinsters/Aunt Lute, 1987. Print.

Baca, Damián. *Mestiz@ Scripts, Digital Migrations and the Territories of Writing.* New York: Palgrave Macmillan, 2008. Print.

Barbershop. MGM Home Entertainment, 2002.

Besa, Andy. Inclusiveness, Exclusivity and Mistaken Identity. AcademiadeCruz. com. 2011, March 21. Web. March 27, 2015.

Drew, Julie. Cultural Composition: Stuart Hall on Ethnicity and the Discursive Turn. In *Race, Rhetoric, and the Postcolonial,* eds. Gary A. Olson and Lynn Worsham, 205–239. Albany: State University of New York Press, 1999. Print.

Enoch, Jessica. Changing Research Methods, Changing History: A Reflection on Language, Location, and Archive. *Composition Studies* 38, no. 2 (2010): 47–73. Print.

Fanon, Frantz. *Black Skin, White Masks,* 1967. Print.

Freire, Paulo. *Pedagogy of the Oppressed.* New York: Bloomsbury Publishing, 2000.

Gómez-Peña, Guillermo. *Dangerous Border Crossers: The Artist Talks Back.* London: Routledge, 2000. Print.

Guzmán, Romeo. Pocho in Greater Mexico's Romeo Guzman. AcademiaDeCruz. com. 2011, March 11. Web, pochoingreatermexico.wordpress.com. March 27, 2015.

Juárez, Marissa. A Chicana Feminist Reflection on What it Means to be Pocha. AcademiaDeCruz.com. 2011, May 20. Web. March 27, 2015.

Kelly, Casey R. Détournement, Decolonization, and the American Indian Occupation of Alcatraz Island (1969–1971). *Rhetoric Society Quarterly* 44, no. 2 (2014): 168–190. Print.

Licona, Adela C. *Zines in Third Space: Radical Cooperation and Borderlands Rhetoric.* Albany: State University of New York Press, 2012. Print.

Lunsford, Andrea A. Toward a Mestiza Rhetoric: Gloria Anzaldúa on Composition and Postcoloniality. *Journal of Advanced Composition* 18, no. 1 (1998): 1–27. Print.

Martinez, Aja Y. 'The American Way': Resisting the Empire of Force and Color-Blind Racism. *College English* 71, no. 6 (2009): 584–595. Print.

Martinez, Aja Y. Three Generations Pocha. AcademiaDeCruz.com. 2011, March 31. Web. March 27, 2015.

Martínez, Natalie. Poch@ as Queer Racial Melancholia. AcademiaDeCruz.com. 2011, June 7. Web. March 27, 2015.

Medina, Cruz, ed. *Academia de Cruz Medina.* www.academiadecruz.com. Web.

Medina, Cruz. Tweeting Collaborative Identity: Race, ICTs and Performing *Latinidad.* In *Communicating Race, Ethnicity, and Identity in Technical*

Communication, eds. Miriam Williamson and Octavio Pimentel, 63–86. Amityville: Baywood Publishing, 2014. Print.

Medina, Cruz. *Reclaiming Poch@ Pop: Examining the Rhetoric of Cultural Deficiency* (Latino Pop Culture Series). New York: Palgrave Macmillan, 2015. Print.

Mejía, Jaime Armín. Rhetoric of Aztlán. Rhetoric Society of America, San Antonio, TX, 2014 May. Conference presentation.

Mi Familia: My Family. New Line Home Video, 1995.

Mignolo, Walter D. Delinking. *Cultural Studies* 21, no. 2. (2007): 449–514. Print.

Moraga, Cherrie, and Gloria Anzaldúa, eds. *This Bridge Called My Back: Writings by Radical Women of Color*. New York: Kitchen Table, Women of Color Press, 1983. Print.

Newcomb, William W. A Reappraisal of the "Cultural Sink" of Texas. *Southwestern Journal of Anthropology* 12, no. 2 (1956): 145–153. Print.

Paredes, Américo, and Richard Bauman. *Folklore and Culture on the Texas-Mexican Border*. Austin, TX: CMAS Books, Center for Mexican American Studies, University of Texas at Austin, 1993. Print.

Powell, Malea. Rhetorics of Survivance: How American Indians Use Writing. *College Composition and Communication* (2002): 396–434.

Powell, Malea. Dreaming Charles Eastman: Cultural Memory, Autobiography, and Geography in Indigenous Rhetorical Histories. In *Beyond the Archives: Research as a Lived Process*, eds. Kirsch and Rohan, 115–128. Carbondale: Southern Illinois University Press, 2008. Print.

Reynoso, Enrique. Phenomenology and Etymology of a Fresa. AcademiaDeCruz.com. 2011, March 23. Web. March 27, 2015.

Rodriguez, Richard. *Hunger of Memory: The Education of Richard Rodriguez: An Autobiography*. Boston: D. R. Godine, 1982. Print.

Ruecker, Todd. Here They Do This, There They Do That: Latinas/Latinos Writing Across Institutions. *College Composition and Communication* 66, no. 2, 2014. Print.

Smith, Linda Tuhiwai. *Decolonizing Methodologies: Research and Indigenous Peoples*. New York: Zed Books, 1999.

Smitherman, Geneva. *Black Talk: Words and Phrases from the Hood to the Amen Corner*. Boston: Houghton Mifflin, 2000. Print.

Spivak, Gayatri Chakravorty. Can the Subaltern Speak? In *Marxism and the Interpretation of Culture*, eds. Cary Nelson and Laurence Grossberg, 217–313. Chicago: University of Illinois Press, 1988. Print.

Thiong'O, Ngugi Wa. *Decolonizing the Mind: The Politics of Language in African Literature*. London: J. Currey, 1986.

Velasco, Juan. Hunger of Memory. *Latino/a Literature in the Classroom: 21st Century Approaches to Teaching*, ed. Frederick Aldama, 291–294. New York: Routledge, 2015. Print.

Villanueva, Victor. *Bootstraps: From an American Academic of Color.* Urbana, IL: National Council of Teachers of English, 1993. Print.

Villanueva, Victor. On the Rhetoric and Precedents of Racism. *College Composition and Communication* 50 (1999): 645–661. Print.

Villarreal, José A. *Pocho.* Garden City, NY: Doubleday, 1959. Print.

Wilson, William E. A Note on 'Pochismo'. *The Modern Language Journal* 30, no. 6 (1946): 345–346. Print.

CHAPTER 8

Mestizaje

Gabriela Raquel Ríos

In this chapter, I highlight an ongoing debate about *mestizaje*'s decolonial and/or liberatory potential from the disciplinary perspectives of Latin American, Chicanx,[1] and Indigenous Studies. I focus on these intersections and overlaps because most discussions of *mestizaje* in the discipline of rhetoric and composition stem from Gloria Anzaldúa's work, which is situated in Chicanx Studies. Additionally, these fields take up decolonial theory most explicitly in their discussions about mestizaje. I then show how the uptake of *mestizaje* in Rhetoric and Composition Studies has led to a recurring set of problematics that have been a source of tension between American Indians and Chicanxs *as well as* Mexican *indígenas* who have migrated into the United States. Moreover, the debate around mestizaje also brings to the fore discursive/materialist tensions on how we discuss power–knowledge relations[2] in rhetoric and composition.

As Chicanxs and others have struggled to articulate our own intellectual traditions through the trope of *mestizaje* to a discipline dominated by Western intellectual traditions, we have often unwittingly reified the racial dynamics through which *mestizaje* functions, both epistemologically and ontologically. Nevertheless, we also use this category to resist the

G.R. Ríos (✉)
Department of English, University of Oklahoma, Norman, OK, USA

© The Editor(s) (if applicable) and The Author(s) 2016
I.D. Ruiz, R. Sánchez (eds.), *Decolonizing Rhetoric and Composition Studies*, DOI 10.1057/978-1-137-52724-0_8

stigmatization and subjugation of "*Othered*" ways of being and knowing. Ultimately, I believe there are productive points of tension *and* overlap in how decolonial theory is used in Chicanx and Indigenous and Latin American Studies. What's more, I believe rhetoric and composition has much to contribute to and learn from these discussions.

MATERIALITY AND POETICS: MESTIZAJE AS A TROPE OF NATIONAL INVENTION

During the revolutionary period in many Latin American countries, indigeneity came to be defined by governing forces through the notion of blood quantum. Additionally, it became synonymous with "primitivism" and "savageness." As such, Indigenous people and Indigenous *cultures* were deemed antithetical to "progress." Nevertheless, the high rates of miscegenation in Latin America created a different kind of "Indian Problem" than the one faced by its neighbors in the United States and Canada. The so-called "rampant mixing" of various now-racialized people led prominent political figures of the nineteenth and twentieth centuries to strategically construct a national *mestizo* subject through the concepts of *indigenismo* and *mestizofilia*.

Mexican scholars such as Jorge José Gómez-Izquierdo have argued that from 1910 on *mestizofilia* became a way to account for and show value in Mexico's racial and cultural heterogeneity while nevertheless homogenizing it through the eugenicist logic of "mixed-race" superiority. In a broader approach to the topic, Olivia Gall's *Racismo, Mestizaje y Modernidad* argues that the trope of *mestizaje* was used by elites as a way to erase or marginalize not only the Indigenous but also the Black population in Latin America and the United States.

In Mexico and elsewhere, José Vasconselos's *raza cosmica* and Manuel Gamio's "integrationist" politics were two of the more prominent logics used to justify the forced removal of *Indigenas* into *ejidos* (or reserves) *while simultaneously* justifying *mestizos*' claim to land, based not only on their "Indian blood" but also on their racial superiority as "mixed-bloods." An important part of constructing the "Mexican Mestizo Nation," then, becomes to "civilize the Indian within," the *national* subject, which is decidedly not the Indian subject: "To incorporate the Indian let us not try to 'Europeanize' him all at once; to the contrary, let us 'indianize' ourselves a bit [...] [n]aturally, we should not exaggerate to a ridiculous degree our closeness with the Indian" (quoted in Saldaña-Portillo 211).

DECOLONIAL APPROACHES TO MESTIZAJE

Decolonial approaches to *mestizaje* vary, but I focus on two particular decolonial perspectives and genealogies for *mestizaje*, one stemming from Latin American Studies and one from Chicanx/Indigenous Studies.[3] The current status of *mestizaje* in both areas is contested, particularly because of differences in how it is taken up differently through decolonialism by each.

Decoloniality in Latin American Studies: Epistemic Options

Although she did not necessarily see it as decolonial or even postcolonial, Gloria Anzaldúa's work on *mestizaje* has become foundational for decolonial theory in Latin American Studies and for many Chicanx scholars. According to Anzaldúa, her new articulation of the consciousness of the *mestiza* explodes the logic of racial and cultural purity built into *mestizaje* in its colonial formations. The new *mestiza* does not simply respond to the colonial logic of *mestizaje* through the familiar Hegelian dialectic; rather, the new *mestiza* consciousness transforms the logic of colonial *mestizaje* by allowing for plurality and complexity, even ambiguity. Her orientation to *mestizaje* challenges the ways it was originally used to exclude certain peoples from power and resources by recognizing our interconnectedness to other peoples and to nonhuman beings and objects:

> The work of *mestiza* consciousness is to break down the subject/object duality that keeps her prisoner. [...] [T]he answer to the problem between the white race and the colored, between males and females, lies in healing the split that originates in the very foundation of our lives, our culture, our languages, our thoughts. (80)

In this way, Anzaldúa argues that her new *mestiza* consciousness opens up possibilities rather than foreclosing them, and it creates a "tolerance for ambiguity" that can be transformed *subconsciously* in an intimate way/location.

For Anzaldúa, this process is a spiritual one by which "the possibility of uniting all that is separate occurs" in order to create a third element "which is greater than the sum of its severed parts" (101–102). This third element is a *mestiza* consciousness. Thus, Anzaldúa challenges Western knowledge formations, such as the subject–object split *and* binary oppositions, that she argues have sustained various forms of oppression. In his important work on critical uses of race in Chicanx culture, Rafael Pérez-Torres argues this kind of "cultural mixture—premised on the lived practices of racial mixture—serves to achieve a change of those people and communities involved" (48).

Emma Pérez' crucial work in a "decolonial imaginary" likewise sees Anzaldúa's conception of *mestizaje* as one that problematizes a colonial inscription about "purity" of blood, of culture, even of sexuality (26). Pérez's thinking advocates for a local history of Chicana feminism that rejects the subject–object dichotomy and offers a way to make Chicana forms of knowledge *visible* options for "future possibilities."

Walter Mignolo's decolonial theory in Latin American Studies has heavily influenced Chicanx studies. Mignolo first began articulating his theory of decoloniality in *The Darker Side of the Renaissance*, where he began a line of inquiry into the semiotic dimensions of coloniality starting in the sixteenth century. Although many Postcolonial or Subaltern Studies' scholars locate a colonial legacy within economic or historical structures alone, Mignolo introduces "colonial semiosis" as both a field and a concept—one that contemplates colonial economies and colonial histories and that "implies the coexistence of interactions among and cultural production by members of radically different cultural traditions" (8, 9). Later, in *Local Histories/Global Designs*, he posits "border thinking" as that which can illuminate the invisible logic of coloniality embedded in modernity (3).

This concept is heavily influenced by Anzaldúa's *mestiza* consciousness, and like Anzaldúa, Mignolo argues that thinking from the colonial wound (or as Anzaldúa would say, the *herida abierta*) can change both the terms and the content of the conversation about colonialism and its ongoing legacies. Racial formations such as *mestizaje* are a product of colonial design insofar as they are predicated in *descriptions* of blood mixture or skin color that are biologized and racialized. Whereas Mignolo eschews mestizaje in its racial formation, in *The Darker Side of Western Modernity* he nevertheless advocates Anzaldúa's "*conciencia de la mestiza*" and even Rodolfo Kusch's formulation of "*mestizo* consciousness" (which, Mignolo admits, is perhaps better understood as "immigrant consciousness" given

Kusch's German background). He treats both as "diverse expressions and experiences of the same condition of existence: *the awareness of coloniality of being*" and as "different modes of experiencing the colonial wound and of engaging the decolonial option" (108, 109).

In reframing the conversation in this way, Mignolo argues it is necessary to understand colonialism from the perspective of subaltern, colonial subjects in order to make visible their "subjugated knowledges"—a term he borrows from Foucault—and to see them as decolonial options (*Local* 20). For Mignolo, it is important to understand these as "options" and not alternatives or other truths because to do so accepts that there is "*a* modernity and *a* development to which nothing but alternatives could exist" (*Western* xxviii–xxix).

In short, the decolonial theories of Pérez and Mignolo aim to *expose* the logic of coloniality in order to better illuminate decolonial options. Anzaldúa's new mestiza consciousness presents one option for undoing the epistemic damage of colonialism and for making visible the histories and diverse knowledges that have been subjugated by colonial designs.

Decoloniality in Indigenous Studies: The Problem of Settler Colonialism

Rather than focus on coloniality, decolonial perspectives in Indigenous Studies tend to emphasize settler colonialism. The difference simultaneously is subtle and not-so subtle. Whereas writers in Latin American Studies, such as Mignolo and Pérez, see decolonization as primarily discursive[4] and/or epistemological and implicitly "future"-focused, writers in Indigenous Studies see decolonization as being primarily about sovereignty; they argue for colonial impact to be acknowledged and *dismantled*. What's more, colonial impact is seen most prominently as one having to do with territorial claims (e.g., to land, knowledge, representations, etc.) and, as such, as having to do with settler subjects and Indigenous subjects, even on a hemispheric or global level. Although these categories are certainly understood as discursively defined, scholars of Indigenous Studies nevertheless recognize that settler nations continue to rob the resources (e.g., land-based, cultural, knowledge, and otherwise) of peoples who are marked as Indigenous by the state. They also see this project as one predicated on the ongoing genocide or disappearance of these indigenous subjects (e.g., see Audra Simpson's *Mohawk Interruptus*).

In looking to "unsettle" the logics of colonialism, Indigenous Studies scholars offer a similar perspective to that of Latin American Studies scholars. However, as Indigenous Studies has taken on a more hemispheric approach, the field has critiqued *mestizaje* as a logic born of modernity, claiming that it constitutes settler-subjects over and against Indigenous subjects. Similarly, Dylan Miner argues that while scholars like Anzaldúa attempt to write from indigenist perspectives, they "are never fully situated in dialogue with tribal epistemologies or ontologies" (218). In addition, as stated previously, the *indigenist* turn in Chicanx Studies has also disavowed *mestizaje*, or at least problematized it. For example, Lourdes Alberto argues that Ana Castillo's *Mixquiahuala Letters* constructs a *mestizo* consciousness that "needs the *unchanging ruins* of indigeneity in order to operate as a dynamic subject position" in order to expose the privilege of *mestizaje* as a logic that constructs the Chicana as "a universal subject that can access both the Indian and the colonial" but only through the silencing of the Native woman (44, emphasis added).

This tension exists, as George Hartley argues, not only because we "uncritically accep[t] the nation-state as arbiter of indigenous status," but also (perhaps paradoxically) because we do not account for it (56). In other words, it is often because Chicanxs do not or cannot account for *how* nation-states structure and define indigeneity in ways that should be challenged or superseded in our *reclamations* of a mode of being, which has been taken from us, that we end up angering American Indian people and Mexican *indígenas* when we lay claims to land through Indigenous lineage or ancestry (i.e., Aztlan).

Finally, Andrea Smith's important critique of indigeneity as a borderland highlights how Gloria Anzaldúa and others have constructed a "new *mestiza* consciousness" that "illuminates how to enact a (border) crossing from marginalized other to whole woman who constantly shifts, crosses, and gains power from contradiction and ambiguity," a phenomenon that occurs as well in mixed-blood constructions in American Indian Studies, "in which 'mixed-blood' identity attains a teleological status as the new and improved indigenous identity, as though indigenous identity in and of itself is incapable of addressing the challenges and complexity of contemporary life" ("Against the Law"). Smith's critique recognizes how Anzaldúa's mestizaje operates according to a logic of modernity (i.e., of futurity and progress) that cannot include indigeneity.

MESTIZ@ RHETORICS

Part of the tension between such perspectives toward decoloniality stems from identity politics and their material impact. In some ways, this tension is linked theoretically to tensions between discursive and materialist critiques of power.

For both Latin American and Indigenous Decolonial Studies, rhetoric (and writing or literacy) are crucial facets of colonialism and its legacy. For example, Mignolo shows that part of the epistemic quality of colonialism is its privileging of alphabetic literacy and denouncing of sophist rhetorical traditions (*Local Histories/Global Designs*). In Indigenous Studies, scholars such as Andrea Smith argue that a crucial component of colonial legacy is ethnographic entrapment, whereby the Indigenous (and other marginalized peoples) are rendered arhetorical and, thus, put in a position to be seen only as objects of knowledge rather than as sovereign intellectuals ("Ethnographic Entrapment").

It would seem, therefore, that Rhetoric and Composition Studies is a site ripe with decolonial potential. Many in our discipline have turned to mestizaje for thinking about colonialism in some liberatory way. Andrea Lundsford introduced Anzaldúa to the discipline to bring postcolonial (if not decolonial) studies into Composition, and since then, scholars, such as Angela Haas, Damián Baca, and Cristina D. Ramirez, have attempted more rigorously to engage "Mestiz@" rhetorics in their decolonial potential. In all of these moments, we have taken to the epistemic quality of *mestizaje* through identity or culture in some way and/or in relation to nation-building.

Baca's book, *Mestiz@ Scripts, Digital Migrations, and the Territories of Writing*, for example, uses the concept of *mestizaje* to examine what he calls "new" literacies. Additionally, in a characteristically *mestizo* process, these new literacies create a *mezcla* (mixture) of European writing and "Aztec" imaging practices, which render (sometimes implicitly and sometimes explicitly) indigeneity and Indigenous culture as the "old" and the mestiz@ the new. Although Baca claims that he does not place Indigenous peoples who have recognized tribal affiliation in the United States within the "Mestiz@" continuum, he nonetheless does place the remainder of the "intellectual province of Mesoamerica" within that continuum (2).[5]

In this vein Baca is inadvertently rehearsing a familiar narrative of modernity and logic of coloniality—the "mixed" or "hybrid" subject and cultures represent a "new," more advanced civilization that comes to *be* in that familiar universal/particular dialectic, wherein Chicanxs become the "universal" subject. However, for Baca—and for many Chicanxs and other Indigenous people—the project of nation-building is still crucial for a decolonial project. This is *partly* because of the ongoing occupation of Native lands by an "outsider" in US and Canadian areas, where Chicanxs and other Indigenous peoples have theorized decolonization.

In her article on "forging a *mestiza* rhetoric," Christina Ramirez articulates a similar concern. Taking a feminist stance, her work uses Anzaldúa's and Baca's work to highlight the ways in which the project of *mestizaje* in Mexico was also a gendered and sexualized project. Her work also recognizes the role that *writing*, in particular, played in construction of national Mexican subjects; additionally, she shows how women were often marginalized in these constructions because of their limited access to public platforms and public discourses. In looking to Mexican women journalists' writing during the time of Mexico's revolution, however, she argues that Mexican women nationals articulated a national identity that was more inclusive than dominant, patriarchal articulations. For example, she argues that the women writers of the *Violetas de Anahuac* used a *mestiza* rhetoric that "blurred the magazines first two purposes—that of contributing to national progress and that of constructing a national identity—with another purpose: forwarding feminism" (614).

Nevertheless, as Ramirez shows, some of these women eschewed this frame, as it was part of a colonial discourse of nation-building at the time (621). However, she argues that a "contemporary" notion of *mestizaje* is more "inclusive" because it resists assimilation. Similarly, Jay Dolmage finds Anzaldúa's reclamation of the word *mestiza* to be generative, not so much because it allows for inclusivity but because rhetorically it challenges the history of denigration attached to *mestiza* bodies, suggesting *mestiza* rhetorics "can always be inherently subversive, embodied, powerfully Other modes of persuasion, even while they have most often been represented as opposite" (224).

While I understand Baca's, Ramirez's, and Dolmage's claims, I think it important to pay closer attention to why these women—and why many women today—resist thinking about themselves, their culture, and their intellectual practices as "*mestiza*." Doing so will help us better understand and somehow address the ongoing tension between Chicanxs and American Indian scholarship and practice and, in turn, consider its implications for Rhetoric and Composition Studies.

TENSIONS AND OVERLAP IN DECOLONIAL APPROACHES TO MESTIZAJE[6]

Even though these two approaches to mestizaje seem hoplessly at odds, I believe that they ultimately come together in fruitful ways. Nevertheless, I think it is important to locate the (fruitful) moments of tension in order to better account for the fruitful moments of overlap. Such tensions exist in how scholars come to understand the colonial problem, power relationships, and the politics of identity.

The Colonial Problem

Latin American theorists who espouse *mestizaje* as decolonial do so because they tend to see the problem of colonialism as something having more to do with modernity than with Indigenous subjects or even indigeneity as a concept. In other words, at its core, colonialism is a product of modernity that has been in the making since the Enlightenment. What's more, as Linda Alcoff points out, for Mignolo the epistemic effects of colonialism are its most damaging and least understood (80).

Coloniality, therefore, is about how power-knowledge is used to define and establish colonial relations among people, land, and so on. Still, the decolonial option does not seek to resist or undo colonial (knowledge) designs so much as it seeks to expose or make visible the designs that have been subjugated by the colonial matrix of power. In the latter case, border thinking and decoloniality are important so as not to reinstate the colonial conditions of possibility with different content. Border thinking is what allows us to understand how the rhetoric (or the epistemology) of modernity hides not only the ways in which development exists only at the cost of lives, but also the many differing forms of knowledge available to us as we (re)design our relationships to one another, to land, and so on. For Mignolo, *mestiza/o* consciousness is one option because it stems from the colonial wound and because it challenges the colonial impulse toward homogeneity—that is, it allows for plurality.

Perez's articulation of "hidden" histories of women in the formation of Mexican nationals, along with Ramirez's similar accounting of Mexican women journalists, also see the problem of colonialism as having to do with homogeneity and purity. These scholars see decolonial potential in *mestizaje's* ability to account for how women and other marginalized people's *histories* are undervalued because they resist the homogenizing tendencies of colonialism. Thus, these formations of decolonial thinking do not necessarily seek to resist or undo colonial formations so much as they hope to expose the many formations of futurity and progress that it seeks to dominate or hide.

In contrast, Indigenous Studies scholars see the colonial problem as one that is fundamentally about the Indigenous subject and/or indigeneity and the settler subject. These scholars also find it necessary to resist and dismantle the structures that sustain settler-colonialism. They argue not only that the genocide of indigenous subjects is at the core of colonialism, but also that so too is the need for settler subjects to "indigenize" themselves through and with the Indigenous subject. Most of these scholars see *mestizaje* as one mechanism by which this project is made manifest. For there to be a "mixed" culture, subject, and knowledge, there must be a "pure" culture, subject, knowledge with which to mix. Additionally, in *mestizaje* the indigenous portion of the mixture is fixed in time and space, whereas the hybrid or mixed subject gains futurity and teleological status.

Power has more to do with access to resources and cultural capital in Indigenous Studies' decolonial approaches to mestizaje. Moreover, sovereignty and nation-building are also equally important to these approaches that see mestizaje as something irrevocably linked to colonial nation-building regimes.

The Politics of Identity and Power Relations

Perhaps at the core of these tensions is the problem of identity politics— and it is here that I find a fruitful overlap and hopefully room for more dialogue—between Latin American and Chicanx/Indigenous Studies' decolonial approaches to *mestizaje*. Mignolo's restructuring of the universal/particular dilemma as a modern/colonial problem in many ways helps us push past identity politics, even though he still sees identity politics as "another [decolonial] option" (*Darker* 137). In fact, his use of the "universal/particular" dilemma is in part a way to move away from identity politics. Nevertheless, there is some slippage in Mignolo's discussion of identity, as Alcoff points out: "On the one hand he shies away from identity politics, but then again he articulates a form of it when he makes such claims as 'for those whom colonial legacies are real (i.e. they hurt) that they are more (logically, historically, and emotionally) inclined than others to theorize the past in terms of coloniality'" (99).

In his most recent book, published after Alcoff's piece, Mignolo explains that he does not eschew identity but rather recognizes how many Indigenous groups have found *identity in politics* to be a more ethical and inclusive model of politics. This strategy resists the liberal tendency to remove identity from politics entirely, which results in "objectivity without identity" (*Darker* 137). Of course, objectivity without identity is a falsity—objectivity has often been ascribed to the unmarked categories of maleness, whiteness, able-bodiedness, and so on. Miner, following George Lipsitz, offers a similar take that draws identity from politics so as to acknowledge "the need to connect research to action and develop collective identities rooted in radical political orientations, as opposed to fixating on identity politics" (217). For Miner, however, this is decidedly a move away from *mestizaje*, which he argues (along with Jack Forbes and Saldaña-Portillo) is so deeply implicated in colonialism that it cannot offer any effective political gain.

Miner's response here is similar to Smith's regarding the concept of "subjectless critique" that has become a powerful and useful corrective to identity politics. According to Smith, queer theory's subjectless critique is important insofar as it resists ethnographic entrapment, which scholars across Latin American and Chicanx and Indigenous Studies agree is a product of colonial design. Additionally, it allows us to resist normalizing logics and discourses based on "inclusion without transformation." Much like Mignolo, however, she argues that subjectless critique has the potential to (and often does) reinstate a normalized subject even while disavowing it. In fact, Smith argues that even a queer of color orientation to *mestizaje* seems to do just that. What disappears in a subjectless critique is the ongoing occupation of Native lands and the genocide of Native peoples. In short, subjectless critique and postidentity stances have the potential to "disappear" the Native subject. Additionally, it operates on a kind of agency for opting out (or, perhaps in Mignolo's case, for opting in) that Indigenous peoples and others who face material conditions of starvation, violence, or war do not possess.

In other words, while Mignolo does believe that there are those for whom the experiences of a colonial legacy are "real," he nonetheless seems to think these people's experiences can be easily reduced and, perhaps, harmoniously aligned with those for whom the colonial legacy is less direct. Nevertheless, *mestizaje* has been and continues to be a source of tension between Chicanxs, American Indians, and even many Mexican *indígenas*, primarily because Anzaldúa simultaneously marks herself as distinct from "*lo indio*" while at the same time biologically linking herself to "*lo indio*" in a familiar eugenicist and biopolitical logic used by Mexican nationals. Additionally, the *mestiza* consciousness represents a "better" or more "advanced" state of being. It is also important to consider that *mestizaje* continues to be a source of oppression and exclusion more so than a source of liberation in social uses among Indigenous groups in Latin America (see Marisol de la Cadena's *Indigenous Mestizos* and Beatriz Reyes-Foster's "Grieving for *Mestizaje*").

In many ways, this tension is linked to materialist and discursive orientations to identity and to the ways we tend to separate the material from the discursive. We are left with troubling, conflicting, and contradictory stances in relation to *mestizaje*—that is, either we locate indigeneity and Indigenous peoples vis-à-vis racist, eugenicist state-sanctioned logics or we locate it vis-à-vis racist, eugenicist biological logics. Both matter (however paradoxically) for the same reason: (ongoing) genocide. One corrective might be, as Miner suggests, that we simply claim our identities through our politics, and that we align ourselves with Indigenous epistemologies and ontologies.

In practice, the very notion of *mestizaje*—and perhaps also of hybridity more generally—rather than exploding the logics of "purity" (i.e., of race, of culture, etc.) actually reifies them because it relies on "pure" subjects that then "mix" to create the mixed "mestiza consciousness" that is ultimately superior to its "parts." Additionally, it highlights that as much as modernity has to do with development, it also has to do with the erasure of Indigenous people. In other words, even though the *mestiza* becomes visible, she does so only at the expense of the Indigenous.

CONCLUSION AND IMPLICATIONS

My discussion by no means exhausts all considerations regarding *mestizaje*. Instead, I have tried to tease out the recurring tensions of *mestizaje* as it has been taken up in various decolonial projects and, particularly, as these projects relate to indigeneity. Although my own politics are aligned with Miner's and those of others who disavow the term entirely, I nevertheless hesitate to tell people how to make sense of their own lived experiences; many seem to find some measure of safety or even liberation in the idea of *mestizaje*. What's more, I think it has helped some of us make sense of a mixed experience. As scholars of Rhetoric and Composition who are invested in decolonial thought, we should be mindful of how the logics of *mestizaje* influence or affect our discussions about cultural practices connected to writing or rhetoric. For example, in their collection, *Mestizo Genomics*, Peter Wade, Carlos López Beltrán, and Eduardo Restrepo note that to talk about genetics and DNA with regard to *mestizaje* is not necessarily to speak about race; however, as Mignolo suggests, our interpretations of genetic findings and our descriptions of biological makeup can be racist when they follow the logics of the racialized discourses of *mestizaje*.

There are at least three problematic tendencies tied to *mestizaje* (and indigeneity) that directly affect Rhetoric and Composition scholarship: (1) the romanticizing and fetishizing of Indigenous cultural practices, including writing, (2) the erasure of indigenous futurity, and (3) the pure/mixed fallacy. Such tendencies must be resisted when we discuss rhetorical practices because *mestizaje* often renders the Indigenous subject arhetorical and fixed in time. These tendencies also become important when we discuss writing, which has been and continues to be connected to our defintions of legibility, visibility, and rhetorical agency.

Definitions of writing matter because they are often deeply embedded in racialized discourses about civility and competence, knowledge, and power. For example, when we suggest that Chicanx students should be valued in education because our practices are "advanced" or are somehow more legitimate because they are born of *mestizaje*, we are advancing colonial logics that mark indigeneity as fixed in time, "pure," and "simple." Moreover, when we suggest that mestiz@ practices represent all Indigenous practices, we "unsee" the ongoing practices of other Indigenous subjects and the struggles they face. Even when we use *mestizaje* as a way to account for the "mixture" of cultural practices in Latin America—including language and writing practices—we reify the logics of cultural and biological purity.

In addition, we cannot forget that educational systems are a colonial construct, developed in part to "civilize" the peoples of this hemisphere, to force the Indigenous population to fall in line with Eurocentric values. This process was (and still is, in many ways) violent and traumatic. *Mestizaje* functions as a mechanism by which educational institutions could help cultivate a proper, civilized national subject. Thus, I follow Miner's and others' examples because I believe responsible approaches to *mestizaje* either disavow the term entirely or—at the very least–disavow its universalizing, racist, and reductive tendencies.

NOTES

1. I use *Chicanx* and *Latinx* because they are used in public/activist discourses as terms that are gender neutral and can therefore include those who do not fall neatly into either side of a gender binary. See Bella Hernandez's "Latinx and Chicanx Identity" for a more thorough explanation. However, when I refer to its use in a particular text, I defer to the author's spelling.
2. *Mestizaje* is actually something imbued with cultural, racialized, and gendered meaning as well as with notions about sexuality and ability (the latter more so in Anzaldúa's articulation of it).
3. My coupling of Chicanx and Indigenous here recognizes the indigenist turn in Chicanx Studies.
4. I do not mean to suggest that these writers see the discursive nature of colonialism as something divorced from materiality. Rather, I see scholars of Latin American Studies orienting themselves to the study of the material effects of discursive formations.
5. Mesoamerica extends from Mexico to Honduras, but because the United States has colonized parts of Mexico, Mesoamerica can be said to include US parts, including areas of Texas, New Mexico, Arizona, and California.
6. I want to stress that my work is inevitably reductive and by no means is an attempt at an exhaustive rendering of decolonial approaches to mestizaje. In keeping with the spirit of Miner's work, I hope this chapter simply offers one perspective that can be put into a dialogue with that of others.

WORKS CITED

Alberto, Lourdes. Topographies of Indigenism: Mexico, Decolonial Indigenism, and the Chicana Transnational Subject in Ana Castillo's *Mixquiahuala Letters.* In *Comparative Indigeneities of the Américas: Toward A Hemispheric Approach,* eds. M. Bianet Castellanos, Lourdes Gutiérrez Nájera, and Arturo J. Aldama Tucson, 38–52. U of Arizona P, 2012. Print.
Alcoff, Linda Martín. Mignolo's Epistemology of Coloniality. *CR: The New Centennial Review* 7, no. 3 (2007): 79–101. Print.
Anzaldúa, Gloria. *Borderlands/La Frontera: The New Mestizaje.* San Francisco: Aunt Lute Books, 1987. Print.
Cadena, Marisol. *Indigenous Mestizos: The Politics of Race and Culture in Cuzco, 1919–1991.* Durham: Duke UP, 2000. Print.
Castellanos M. Bianet, Lourdes Gutiérrez Nájera, and Arturo J. Aldama, eds. *Comparative Indigeneities of the Américas: Toward A Hemispheric Approach.* Tucson: U of Arizona P, 2012. Print.
Gall, Olivia. *Racismo, Mestizaje y Modernidad: Visones desde latitudes diversas.* Mexico City: Universidad Autonoma de Mexico. Print.

Gamio, Manuel. *Forjando Patria: Pro-Nacionalismo.* Trans. Fernando Armstrong-Fumero. Boulder: U of Colorado P, 2010. Print.

Gómez-Izquierdo, Jorge José. Racismo y Nacionalismo en el Discurso de las Élites Mexicanas. In *Caminos del Racismo en México,* ed. Jorge José Gómez Izquierdo, 117–181. Mexico City: Plaza y Valdés. Print.

Hartley, George. Chican@ Indigeneity, The Nation-State, and Colonialist Identity Formations. In *Comparative Indigeneities of the Américas: Toward A Hemispheric Approach,* eds. M. Bianet Castellanos, Lourdes Gutiérrez Nájera, and Arturo J. Aldama Tucson, 53–66. U of Arizona P, 2012. Print.

Hernández, Roberto. Running for Peace and Dignity: From Traditionally Radical Chicanas/os to Radically Traditional Xicanas/os. In *Latin@s in the World System: Decolonization in the Twenty-First Century U.S. Empire,* eds. Ramón Grosfugel, Nelson Maldonado-Torrez, and José David Saldivár. Boulder, CO: Paradigm, 2005. Print.

Lunsford, Andrea. Toward a Mestiza Rhetoric: Gloria Anzaldúa on Composition and Postcoloniality. *JAC* 18 (1998): 1–27. Print.

Mignolo, Walter D. *Local Histories/Global Designs: Coloniality, Subaltern Knowledges, and Border Thinking.* Princeton: Princeton University Press, 2000. Print.

Mignolo, Walter D. *The Darker Side of the Renaissance: Literacy, Territoriality, and Colonization.* 2nd ed. Ann Arbor: U of Michigan P, 2003. Print.

Mignolo, Walter D. *The Darker Side of Western Modernity: Global Futures, Decolonial Options.* Durham: Duke UP, 2011. Print.

Miner, Dylan. *Creating Aztlan: Chicano Art, Indigenous Sovereignty, and Lowriding Across Turtle Island.* Tucson: U of Arizona P, 2014. Print.

Moraga, Cherríe L. *A Xicana Codex of Changing Consciousness: Writings, 2000–2010.* Durham: Duke UP, 2011. Print.

Perez, Emma. *The Decolonial Imaginary: Writing Chicanas into History.* Indianapolis: Indiana UP, 1999. Print.

Pérez-Torres, Rafael. *Mestizaje: Critical Uses of Race in Chicano Culture.* Minneapolis: U of Minnesota P, 2006. Print.

Ramirez, Cristina D. Forging a Mestiza Rhetoric: Mexican Women Journalists' Role in the Construction of a National Identity. *College English* 71 (2009): 606–629.

Reyes-Foster, Beatriz. Grieving for Mestizaje: Alternative Approaches to Maya Identity in Yucatan, Mexico. *Identities: Global Studies in Culture and Power* 19 (2012): 657–672. Print.

Saldaña-Portillo, María Josefina. *The Revolutionary Imagination in the Americas and the Age of Development.* Durham: Duke UP, 2003. Print.

Simpson, Audra. *Mohawk Interruptus: Political Life Across the Borders of Settler States.* Durham: Duke UP, 2014. Print.

Smith, Andrea. Queer Theory and Native Studies: The Heteronormativity of Settler Colonialism. *GLQ* 16 (2010): 41–68. Print.

Smith, Andrea. Against the Law: Indigenous Feminism and the Nation-State. *Affinities Journal* 5 (2011): n. pag. Web. May 15, 2014.

Vasconselos, José. *The Cosmic Race: A Bilingual Edition.* Trans. Didier T. Jaén. Baltimore: Johns Hopkins UP, 1997.

Wade, Peter. Rethinking Mestizaje: Ideology and Lived Experience. *Journal of Latin American Studies* 37 (2005): 239–257. Print.

Wolfe, Patrick. Settler Colonialism and the Elimination of the Native. *Journal of Genocide Research* 8 (2007): 387–409. Print.

CHAPTER 9

Éxito (Success)

Octavio Pimentel and Nancy Wilson

In 1519, Hernán Cortés embarked on a mission to Mexico as a bearer of civilization, "allegedly a selfless act on the Europeans' part for which 'barbarous'" people should be grateful (Spicer 282). Communicating this "civilizing" information to the indigenous people, however, was problematic because of language differences. To remedy the situation, sons of chiefs were "taken for special instruction into schools away from their homes where in the course of receiving instruction in the subjects of the day they would learn Spanish. This policy definitely did not look toward the learning of Spanish by the general Indian population" (423). Bernal Díaz del Castillo, who accompanied Cortés and whose *Historia Verdadera de la Conquista de la Nueva España* provides a rare glimpse into the details of the mission, recounts that the son of the king of Tezcuco was not only taught Spanish but also was baptized and named after his godfather Hernán Cortés. In exchange, the young man was allowed to keep his high status: *"y luego sin más dilaciones, con gran fiesta y regocijo de todo Tezcuco, le alzaron por rey y señor natural, con todas las ceremonias que a los tales reyes solían hacer, y con mucha paz y en amor de todos sus vasallos y otros pueblos comarcanos, y mandaba muy absolutamente y era obedecido"* (441).

O. Pimentel (✉) • N. Wilson
Department of English, Texas State University, San Marcos, TX, USA

© The Editor(s) (if applicable) and The Author(s) 2016   125
I.D. Ruiz, R. Sánchez (eds.), *Decolonizing Rhetoric and Composition Studies*, DOI 10.1057/978-1-137-52724-0_9

Prince Tezcuco's experience exemplifies Kenyan writer and activist Ngũgĩ wa Thiong'o's likening of colonization to a cultural bomb: the colonized lose "belief in their names, in their language, in their environment, in their heritage of struggle, in their unity, in their capacities and ultimately in themselves" (3). Eventually, the colonized come to view their "past as one wasteland of non-achievement and it makes them want to distance themselves from that wasteland" (3). As Burkholder and Johnson note, "within two generations the upper ranks of the Indian nobility of central Mexico and Peru became racially mixed and culturally Spanish. The general pattern was for the indigenous royal families and great territorial nobles to lose ground or be pushed aside" (190).

More than 500 years later, and despite the presence and popularity of multiculturalism in textbooks (see Banks and Banks; Nieto and Bode), ethnic minorities in the United States still experience the effects of colonization's cultural bomb as they are asked to distance themselves from their names, language, and heritage in order to assimilate to the dominant group—White European Americans (WEAs) (Santa Ana; Shaheen). In the case of Latinxs, this process of assimilation may mean Anglicizing their names, favoring English, and buying into a concept of color-blindness that emphasizes the individual versus the collective. Members of minoritized[1] cultures also are asked to view their pasts as one wasteland of achievement from which they should distance themselves, lest they appear disloyal to the United States.

Still, as Easley, Bianco, and Leech report in "Ganas: A Qualitative Study Examining Mexican Heritage Students' Motivation to Succeed in Higher Education," for immigrant and first-generation Mexican heritage college students, specifically, a strong tether to their families and to their Latinx culture is extremely important. In fact, after examining autobiographies written by 103 students attending a prominent Western university, we found that 46 % of the autobiographies and 48 % of the subsequent interviews contained references to *ganas*, "a deeply held desire to achieve academically fueled by parental struggle and sacrifice" (169). The participants specifically referred to "parental struggle and sacrifice," "strong value of family and family's history," "parental admiration and respect," "desire to repay and pay forward," and "resilience and willingness to persevere" (169).

Therein lies the conflict that we wish to address: Although Latinx students draw support from *ganas*, this perceived reliance on others conflicts directly with the individualistic mentality that characterizes success in the

United States. We believe the answer is to redefine *éxito* (success)—to flip the script and acknowledge rather than impugn the communal strengths of the Latinx culture such as a belief in the concepts of *buena gente, buen trabajador*, and *bien educado*—and to recognize the value of *historias de éxito*. Most important, these terms are already used by those *within* Mexicano communities to arrive at their own decolonized definitions of *éxito*. We simply are acknowledging their value, an act that would benefit WEA culture as well. As Tim Wise observes in *Colorblind: The Rise of Post-Racial Politics and the Retreat from Racial Equity*, only by "resolving to view individuals and communities as they really are—which requires acknowledging their languages, cultures, traditions, and racialized experiences—can we actually build the kind of democracy that treats all persons fairly and equally" (21).

THE SHORTCOMINGS OF WEA INDIVIDUALISM

For some time, scholars have been examining how individuality works within various cultural groups. In *Habits of the Heart*, Robert N. Bellah et al., address what they see as a core conflict in the United States between individuality and community. They claim that individuality is corrupting America's social and moral fabric. They point out that "we have moved from the local life of the nineteenth century—in which economic and social relationships were visible and, however imperfectly, morally interpreted as parts of a larger common life—to a society vastly more interrelated and integrated economically, technically, and functionally" (50). They, however, note that despite such integration, "this is a society in which the individual can only rarely and with difficulty understand himself and his activities as interrelated in morally meaningful ways with those of other, different Americans" (50).

In other words, Americans are often so focused on individual success that they become blind to the benefits of communal social networks. Bellah and his coauthors insist, therefore, that the United States needs to rebuild community and renew the cause of social justice. In fact, in *The Good Society*, Bellah et al. claim that what holds Americans back is their abiding allegiance to individualism—the belief that the "good society" is one in which individuals are left to strive independently to reach the goals that have been set by themselves, not in collaboration with others.

In a similar vein, in *Bowling Alone*, Robert Putnam writes that the decline in Americans' civic and social engagement has almost eliminated community social networks that in the past provided social capital. More specifically, tracing this decline to the 1970s, Putman refers to the lack of social activities (e.g., bowling, playing cards, dinners) that once were very popular in the United States. He explains that "many Americans continue to claim that we are 'members' of various organizations, but most Americans no longer spend much time in community organizations— we've stopped doing committee work, stopped serving as officers, and stopped going to meetings" (64-5). He proposes that both individuals and institutions should have the goal of reinstating the need for social gatherings once again.

The emphasis on individuality that Bellah et al. and Putnam write about exists in many different aspects of life, including social responsibility and economics. According to these authors, the need for individuality pushes White middle-class society toward a bias against people whose main goals are not individual. According to this bias, "anything that would violate our right to think for ourselves, judge for ourselves, make our own decisions, live our lives as we see fit, is not only morally wrong, it is sacrilegious" (Bellah, *Habits* 142). Although there are modes of communal activity (e.g.., church organizations), according to Bellah et al. and Putnam, these are exceptions. As a result, community-oriented concepts are often not valued. This happens in many spaces, including schools where teamwork is professed but individual practices are rewarded, often to the students' confusion. For example, students may be encouraged to work in groups, but when it comes to their grades, each of the individual's work within the group may be evaluated.

The WEA emphasis on individualism is obvious in the concept of color-blindness, which urges us not to see significant differences between a white, black, or brown person. This rhetoric of color-blindness professes that people are individuals before they are members of groups, and that their success can therefore be determined individually rather than through groups. As Wise observes, however:

> [W]e can't all "just be Americans," because we never have been just that. For whites, Americanism was something that could be taken for granted (indeed it was synonymous with their racial group), while for others it has never been something to which they could lay claim as readily. And we can't all "just be individuals," because no one is just that, nor has anyone ever lived as such, anywhere, at any time, on the face of the Earth. The rhetoric of colorblindness and individualism has been around for many years, and it is deeply embedded in US discourse.

For Wise, the primary danger of color-blindness is that it ignores differences in opportunities made available to us.by way of example, he likens skin color to a disability, noting that "no one would ever offer universal solutions for improving life for the disabled, or an 'ability-blind' approach, since to be blind to (dis)ability is to make it impossible to address the very thing that is giving rise to the individual's mistreatment and lesser opportunity in the first place" (20). Although Wise's point is well-taken—glossing over the fact that systemic racism continues to exist does not do anyone a favor—he fails to emphasize the unique *strengths* that those outside of the mainstream (including the disabled) may possess.

By redefining *éxito*, we seek to focus on the positive attributes. Of course, because these terms do not reflect US-style individuality, such ideas of success are commonly misunderstood, misinterpreted, and eventually dismissed by US discourses and institutions. For Mexicano and Latinx scholars, however, these terms are potentially game-changing in that they finally provide a vocabulary that comes *from* the community itself.

EN OTRAS PALABRAS

In *The Power of Latino Leadership*, Juana Bordas specifies *personalismo*, *conciencia*, and *destino* as crucial qualities for Latinx success. In this chapter, however, we focus on the terms that Pimentel has added to this list: *buena gente*, *buen trabajador*, and *bien educado* (*Historias de Éxito*). It is worth considering each of them in order to get a sense of the communal values that produce them.

El primer tema es buena gente. A person is *buena gente* who puts others' desires, needs, goals, and so on in front of his or her own. More specifically, someone is buena gente when willing to help write an article, despite not completing one's own; when lending money to a friend, despite not paying the rent; when giving up a chair to someone despite being tired. The common denominator is the sacrifice this person is willing to make, despite any personal needs. Although often ignored, at least by WEA values, to be *buena gente* is to possess a quality that many Latinx leaders believe is crucial to genuine success.

A *buen trabajador*, or *buena trabajadora*, is a "hard worker." The task at hand does not matter; the reward comes from working hard to complete it. For example, if a mother works two jobs to support her family, she will be identified as a *buena trabajadora* regardless of the jobs she holds because she is doing everything in her power to support her family.

Someone who works meticulously and quickly at Starbucks could also be identified as a *buena trabajadora* because she is "working hard."

A literal translation of *bien educado* is "well educated," but the concept is more complex, thus its beauty. *Para que una persona sea identificada como bien educada es muy difícil y por eso es un honor muy grande para la persona y su familia.* To be identified as a *bien educado* means that someone appreciates your ethos, who you are as a person. Such an description is a great compliment to you and your family, thus highly valued.

Buena gente, buen trabajador, and *bien educado* are community-oriented concepts. They reflect common practices of mexicano communities and are *not* necessarily associated with wealth, individuality, or academic success. Related to them is the idea of an *historia de éxito.* Very much unlike "traditional success stories" that are often embedded within individuality, wealth, or formal education, *historias de éxito* envision success more broadly. They are commonly guided by the values of an individual's social network. For example, a successful Mexican medical doctor whose social network is composed of other doctors might define her *historia de éxito* as the ability to help save the lives of people. Then again, a recent Mexican immigrant whose social networks are composed of other newly arrived immigrants may define her *historia de éxito* as having a job, even though it may be at McDonald's.

In other words, not all citizens of the United States wish to be identified as successful because they have obtained a formal education and wealth, or have pulled themselves up by their bootstraps. Some communities have quite different values. The difference between *historias de éxito* and traditional WEA success stories is that the latter are commonly embedded within notions of individuality; they center on an individual's achievements.

ÉXITO EN LA ESCUELA

Unfortunately, Latinxs in academia may feel conflicted as they attempt to straddle the WEA and Latinx worlds. In fact, in *Latino College Presidents: In Their Own Words,* David J. León and Rubén O. Martinez report that the people they interviewed found discussing their academic lives "the most difficult assignment because it required them to reflect upon their entire life and career while pulling together two disparate worlds: the Latino world of their family and friends, and the Anglo-American one which emphasizes individual achievement" (37). Gloria Anzaldúa casts this "coming together of two self-consistent but habitually incompatible frames of reference" as "*un choque*, a cultural collision" (428). It is important to recognize that the stories of these Latinx college presidents, Anzaldúa, and others serve as the valuable *historias de éxito* previously discussed.

One way of reconciling opposing ideologies is, of course, to conform to the dominant, public one and turn one's back on the private, home community—that is, to become a hegemonic intellectual. According to Aronowitz and Giroux, hegemonic intellectuals "do more than surrender to forms of academic and political incorporation, or hide behind spurious claims to objectivism; they self-consciously define themselves through the forms of moral and intellectual leadership they provide for dominant groups and classes" (39). Colloquially, a hegemonic intellectual may be called an Uncle Tom or a *Tío Taco*.

Richard Rodriguez has been criticized as a hegemonic intellectual for arguing in *Hunger of Memory* that students should not be allowed to use Spanish in school. Rodriguez recalls his life as the son of Mexican immigrants and uses this story to speak directly about the need for US citizens to know English, what he terms "public language," even if this means sacrificing one's "private language" (i.e., Spanish). In fact, he claims:

> Without question, it would have pleased me to hear my teachers address me in Spanish when I entered the classroom. I would have felt much less afraid. I would have trusted them and responded with ease. But I would have delayed—for how long postponed?—having to learn the language of public society. I would have evaded—and for how long could I have afforded to delay?—learning the great lesson of school, that I had a public identity. (*Hunger* 19)

In addition, later Rodriquez notes:

> Only when I was able to think of myself as an American, no longer an alien in gringo society, could I seek the rights and opportunities necessary for full public individuality…. I celebrate the day I acquired my new name. Those middle-class ethnics who scorn assimilation seem to me filled with decadent self-pity, obsessed by the burden of public life. Dangerously, they romanticize public separateness and they trivialize the dilemma of the socially disadvantaged. (27)

Yet Rodriguez admits that in achieving his "American" identity, he left his parents behind.

Tomás Rivera, one of Rodriguez's sharpest critics, writes that whereas "in the Hispanic world, the interior world of *Ser* is ultimately more important than the world of *Estar*," Rodriguez "opts for the *Estar* world as the more important and does not give due importance to the world of *Ser*. He has problems, in short, with the world from which he came. Surely this is an antithesis to a humanistic development" (7–8). Rivera also addresses the fact that Rodriguez likens himself to Caliban from Shakespeare's *The Tempest*. That is, like Caliban who acquires power when he learns Prospero's language, Rodriguez views learning English "like a native" to be key to his own success in the United States. However, Rivera is again highly critical of Rodriguez's willingness, even eagerness, to trade the communal values of his culture for material advancement, asking: "Is Caliban a reflection of a North American education? Is it an indication of an education which refuses to acknowledge as important only that which is tied to the northern European cultures?" (31)

Ironically, in Aimé Césaire's *A Tempest*, Caliban is no longer depicted as an ignorant savage but rather as a colonized native who rebels against the colonizer Prospero. That is, Césaire rewrites Caliban as an organic or transformative intellectual who uses knowledge, not to serve the colonizer but to challenge him. It similarly became the mission of Rivera and other Chicanx writers to underscore the personal and communal cost of selling out one's home culture.

In Luis Valdez's *Los Vendidos*, the ludicrous Miss. JIM-in-ez works for Governor Reagan and cannot speak Spanish, and in Américo Paredes *George Washington Gómez*, protagonist Guálinto changes his name to George G. Gómez, marries an Anglo woman, and becomes a US Army officer tasked with border security; as a result, Guálinto has a "divided personality, made up of tight little cells independent and almost entirely ignorant of each other" (147). Explaining why he omitted Guálinto's university education, Paredes recounts: "[I]t was what I saw at the time. This was before there was any Chicano movement. The LULACS were trying to teach their children not to speak Spanish. They had a law passed saying that Mexicanos were white…. The trend was toward assimilation" (Garza-Falcón 189).

Rather than assimilate to the WEA culture, Norma González, Luis Moll, and Cathy Amanti advocate adopting culturally sensitive pedagogies specifically focusing on funds of knowledge. They mention that it is important for scholars and teachers to meet the students where they are at and not to dismiss the cultural knowledge they bring to the classroom. For example, if a Mexicano student comes to school with an abundance of Spanish language fluency, then the scholar should build on it, using this student's cultural knowledge to enhance his or her academic experience. Pimentel and Pimentel also have written about the need to form coalitions with students in order to decenter WEA culture and center Latinx culture.

Other scholars, such as Perez, further elaborate on the need of brown students to develop relationships with their teachers, writing that "culturally diverse students need a relationship with their teachers that are mutually respectful if they are to learn. They not only need to like their teachers, but also must sense that their teachers care for them" (103). Unfortunately, as Garza, Ovando, and Seymour note, "once students step into the context of the classroom, educators may perceive [the students'] unique assets as problems, complex challenges, or differences that are misinterpreted" (297). This misinterpretation can lead to the common practice of placing such students in remedial or in a lower academic track.

ÉXITO EN EL FUTURO

Mexicans and Mexican Americans are not being identified as successful because they are being evaluated according to a biased rubric that is often unfamiliar to them. For this to stop, we need to encourage brown people to become successful on their own terms, thus helping, perhaps, to minimize the racism they continue to experience. Scholars can help by engaging in research that acknowledges rather than glosses over cultural differences.

It is important to note, however, that the decolonizing process can sometimes be read as taking power back and even as taking revenge. Unfortunately, this understanding of decolonizing feeds back into the WEA notion of success as defined by power and money. Instead, we conceive the decolonizing process as simply refusing to participate in the denigration of one's names, language, environment, heritage of struggle, unity, and capacities (Ngũgĩ 3). In other words, we recommend rejecting the reification that comes with individualism, (false) color-blindness, wealth, and formal schooling.

To that end, we support Wise's recommendation that educators engage students in "'centering' exercises in class that allow students of color to reflect favorably on their identities and values" (181). Specifically, for

Latinxs this would mean embracing the concepts of *buena gente, buen trabajador,* and *bien educado* and to listening to *historias de éxito.* It would be great if we were all equal, if color did not matter, and if we all had an opportunity to reach any goal we had for ourselves. Wouldn't it be *padre, si no importaba si eras mujer, homosexual, de edad,* or had any other -isms. But that is not the way things are. The United States is invested in pushing people to either conform to the WEA version of success or to be *Other*ed. Perhaps the best place to view this practice is in the media. All you have to do is to watch or to read what the media presents. It says: *para que una mujer sea bonita tiene que medir cinco pies con diez pulgadas y pesar ciento quince libras, que para tener exitó tienes que tener una grandisima casa y un carro extra lugoso y una carrera que paga mucho dinero.* But, we have to understand that not all communities wish for these things.

NOTE

1. *Minoritized* is used instead of minority because often the ethnic group is no longer the minority; however, the WEA rhetoric continues to marginalize them.

WORKS CITED

Anzaldúa, Gloria. *La Conciencia de la Mestiza*: Towards a New Consciousness. *American Feminist Thought at Century's End*, ed. Linda S. Kauffman, 427–440. Cambridge: Blackwell, 1993. 427–440. Print.

Aronowitz, Stanley, and Henry Giroux. *Education Under Siege*. London: Routledge, 2003. Print.

Banks, James A., and Cherry A. McGee Banks. *Multicultural Education: Issues and Perspectives*. 8th ed. Hoboken, NJ: Wiley, 2013. Print.

Bellah, Robert N., Richard Madsen, William M. Sullivan, Ann Swidler, and Steven M. Tipton. *Habits of the Heart: Individualism and Commitment in American Life*. New York: Harper & Row, 1985. Print.

Bellah, Robert N., Richard Madsen, Steven M. Tipton, William M. Sullivan, and Ann Swidler. *The Good Society*. New York: Random House, 1992. Print.

Bordas, Juana. *The Power of Latino Leadership: Culture, Inclusion, and Contribution*. San Francisco: Berrett-Koehler, 2013. Print.

Burkholder, Mark A., and Lyman L. Johnson. *Colonial Latin America*. 2nd ed. New York: Oxford UP, 1994. Print.

Césaire, Aimé. *A Tempest*. Trans. Alexandria, VA: Alexander Street P, 2010. Print.

Díaz del Castillo, Bernal. *Historia Verdadera de la Conquista de la Nueva España*. 5th ed. Mexico: Editorial Porrua, 1960. Print.

Easley, Nate Jr., Margarita Bianco, and Nancy Leech. *Ganas*: A Qualitative Study Examining Mexican Heritage Students' Motivation to Succeed in Higher Education. *Journal of Hispanic Higher Education* 11 (2012): 164–178.

Garza, Rubén, Martha N. Ovando, and Claire E. Semour. Latino and White Students' Perceptions of Teacher Behaviors That Convey Caring: Do Gender and Ethnicity Matter? *Current Issues in Education* 13 (2010): 1–31. Print.

Garza-Falcón, Leticia M. *Gente Decente: A Borderlands Response to the Rhetoric of Dominance*. Austin, TX: U of Texas P, 1998. Print.

González, Norma, Luis C. Moll, and Cathy Amanti. Introduction: Theorizing Practices. *Funds of Knowledge: Theorizing Practices in Households, Communities, and Classrooms*, eds. Norma González, Luis C. Moll, and Cathy Amanti, 1–29. Mahwah, NJ: Erlbaum, 2005. Print.

León, David J., and Rubén O. Martinez. *Latino College Presidents: In Their Own Words. Diversity in Higher Education Series*, vol. 13. Bingley, UK: Emerald, 2013. E-book.

Lippi-Green, Rosina. *English With an Accent: Language, Ideology, and Discrimination in the United States*. New York: Routledge, 2012. Print.

Nieto, Sonia, and Patty Bode. *Affirming Diversity: The Sociopolitical Context of Multicultural Education*. New York: Pearson, 2012. Print.

Ngũgĩ wa Thiong'o. *Decolonising the Mind: The Politics of Language in African Literature*. Portsmouth, NH: Heinemann, 1986. Print.

Paredes, Américo. *George Washington Gómez: A Mexicotexan Novel*. Houston: Arte Publico, 1990. Print.

Pimentel, Charise, and Octavio Pimentel. Coalition Pedagogy: Building Bonds Between Instructors and Students of Color. In *Included in English Studies: Learning Climates That Cultivate Racial anddd Ethnic Diversity*, eds. Victor Villanueva and Shelli B. Fowler, 115–124. Washington, DC: American Association of Higher Education, 2002. Print

Pimentel, Octavio. An Invitation to a Too-Long Postponed: Race and Composition. *Reflections: A Journal of Writing, Community Literacy, and Service Learning* 12, no. 2 (2013): 90–104. Print.

Pimentel, Octavio. *Historias de Éxito within Mexican Communities: Silenced Voices*. New York: Palgrave, 2015. Print.

Putnam, Robert D. *Bowling Alone: The Collapse and Revival of American Community*. New York: Simon & Schuster, 2000. Print.

Ramsey, Patricia. *Teaching and Learning in a Diverse World: Multicultural Education for Young Children*. New York: Teachers College P, 2015. Print.

Rivera, Tomás. Richard Rodriguez's *Hunger of Memory* as Humanistic Antithesis. *MELUS* 11, no. 4 (1984): 5–13. Print.

Rodriguez, Richard. *Hunger of Memory: The Education of Richard Rodriguez*. Boston: D.R. Godine, 1982. Print.

Santa Ana, Otto. *Juan in a Hundred: The Representation of Latinos on Network News*. Austin, TX: University of Texas Press, 2013. Print.

Shaheen, Jack. *Reel Bad Arabs: How Hollywood Vilifies a People*. Northampton, MA: Olive Branch Press, 2009. Print.

Spicer, Edward H. *Cycles of Conquest: The Impact of Spain, Mexico, and the United States on Indians of the Southwest, 1533–1960*. Tucson: U of Arizona P, 1967. Print.

Valdez, Luis. *Los Vendidos*. Alexandria, VA: Alexander Street P, 2004. E-book.

Wise, Tim J. *Colorblind: The Rise of Post-Racial Politics and the Retreat from Racial Equity*. San Francisco: City Lights, 2010. Print.

CHAPTER 10

Chicana Feminism

Candace Zepeda

The "nontraditional places" introduced by Chicana Feminist Sonia Saldívar-Hull represent a *Third Space*, a place that provides access to a different way of conceptualizing history—a place for uncovering the hidden and/or silent voices of the marginalized (Sandoval, Pérez):

> Because our work has been ignored by the men and women in charge of the modes of cultural production, we must be innovative in our search. Hegemony has so constructed the ideas of methods and theory that often we cannot recognize anything that is different from what the dominant discourse constructs. As a consequence, we have to look in **nontraditional** places for our theories. (Saldívar-Hull, *Feminism on the Border*, 46)

In the broadest definition, Third Space is a flexible, multidimensional, and postcolonial theoretical term linked to notions of social identity, places, spaces, locality, politics, and geography.

Although Third Space as a theory is often attributed to postmodern male scholars, such as Homi Bhabha, Edward Soja, Michel Foucault, and Henri Lefebvre, this chapter's author propose that it is through the post-

C. Zepeda (✉)
Department of English, Our Lady of the Lake University, San Antonio, TX, USA

© The Editor(s) (if applicable) and The Author(s) 2016
I.D. Ruiz, R. Sánchez (eds.), *Decolonizing Rhetoric and Composition Studies*, DOI 10.1057/978-1-137-52724-0_10

modern scholarship of Chicana Feminism that the complexity of spatiality and Third Space imagination has been refined. Third Space Chicana Feminism contributes to the larger theoretical and methodological platforms of Third World Feminism with the works of Chicana scholars such as Chela Sandoval, Gloria Anzaldúa, Cherríe Moraga, and Emma Pérez. The active engagement of Third Space scholarship, as it relates to the Southwest borderland, borderland consciousness, historical trauma, historiography, testimonial, and modes of differential consciousness, makes the work of Chicana Feminism valuable and distinguishable among Third World Feminism and Third Space scholarship.

Principally, Chicana Feminism collectively responds to and contests the historical dehumanization and marginalization of people of color. In doing so, Chicana feminists provide rhetorical tools that allow for the reinterpretation of normative and fragmented theories, pedagogies, and practices. As a theoretical consciousness, Chicana Feminism recognizes the lived experiences of difference such as race, culture, nation, class, sexual orientation, and gender. As a pedagogy, it reflects on the interrupted hegemonic discourse of the academy and invites the marginalized to participate in the study and rewriting of their fragmented histories; it opens an in-between space for social identity that was not addressed by exclusionary US hegemonic Feminist theory. Consequently, as a practice, Chicana Feminism responds to the dominant form of feminism and writes in opposition to the discourse that recognizes gender as separate from race and class, and in opposition to the academy, which has never fully recognized Chicana feminists as active agents (Córdova 194).

As a practice, Chicana Feminism established a mobility of identity, encouraging a new citizen–subject that articulated a self-conscious production of political and social opposition (Sandoval 76). Chicana feminists' refusal to assimilate within hegemonic feminist praxis is in part what Sandoval defines as their loyalty to a "differential mode of consciousness" that encourages social justice for varying internally colonized communities. It is through this mode of consciousness that Chicana Feminism is enacted, providing a unique discourse (i.e., a "common speech") that empowers Third Space subjects and that generates various ways of knowing Third Space citizens, spaces, and places (Sandoval 45–50). To develop this argument, I outline three central and distinguishable concepts undergirding the theories, pedagogies, and practices of Chicana Feminism, beginning with the study of historical modes of consciousness.

HISTORICAL CONSCIOUSNESS

The first concept contends that Chicana Feminism's theories present an alternative approach for understanding historical consciousness—a theoretical approach grounded in history. One example is how Chicana feminists respond to the ways historians have written about colonized people and places. For such a discussion, I rely on the scholarship of Chicana scholar Chela Sandoval and Chicana historian Emma Pérez.

Sandoval's *Methodology of the Oppressed* provides decolonial and postcolonial theoretical models for the "decoding of cultural artifacts" including Third Space citizens (10). Her critique of Frederic Jameson's 1984 *Postmodernism, or the Cultural Logic of Late Capitalism* is noteworthy because she points out flaws, especially Jameson's inability to recognize new citizen–subjects who ascend from colonization and can transform into new, "more liberatory" cultures and communities (16). Jameson's exclusion of Third Space citizen–subjects in his critique of postmodernism further justifies the need to study Chicana feminists who make visible Third Space subjects.

Sandoval's critique of Jameson is also fundamental for Emma Pérez, who draws attention to Third Space subjects in her postmodern concept of the decolonial imaginary. Pérez conceptualizes the decolonial imaginary as a time-lag between the colonial and the postcolonial. Pérez suggests this lag as a "rupturing space [or] interstitial space where differential politics and social dilemmas are negotiated" (6). By contesting the tradition of history, Pérez's goal is to provide a Third Space—a tool for uncovering the silenced voices of the marginalized, where agency is enacted through the discourse of Chicana Feminism (xvi).

Pérez defines traditional historiography as "the writing and the study of history," a writing in which "theories are constructed" that erase Third Space subjects on their way to becoming "the prominent ideologies of any given area of study" (9). Traditional history produces a fictive past that becomes the knowledge manipulated to repudiate Third Space subjects (xvii). In its place, Pérez advocates for the emergence of a Chicanx historical imagination in which social binaries (e.g., those of class, race, sexual orientation, and/or gender) are contemplated and negated in all areas of study, including theories that respond to Third Space subjects (11).

In other words, Pérez and Sandoval provide alternative theories for understanding how history has been written on the bodies of Mexican

Americans and how history constructs theories and practices for educating those bodies (Pérez xvi, 9). For instance, consider the impact of colonialism on the social class structure of the Southwest, particularly near the US–Mexico borderlands. With colonialism came Euroamericans and Anglocentric ideologies about education entitlement, educational practices and policies, and eventually pedagogies that shaped discursive practices for Spanish-speaking students in schools.

Nevertheless, rarely is the history of education studied through a postcolonial lens to examine how themes of colonization and oppression played a significant part in the evolution of hegemonic ideologies. Because of its exclusionary and oppressive nature, the early US educational system racialized and segregated Third Space subjects. The following section introduces the pedagogical approaches of Chicana feminists and acknowledges how spatiality influences Third Space subjectivity in the classroom.

Spatial Awareness

The second foundational concept of Third Space Chicana Feminism acknowledges how spatiality influences Third Space subjects' dimensions of knowing to include the physical, spiritual, and metaphysical. Studying how the ecological spaces of home and community contribute to Third Space subjects' epistemological development also can provide insight on how Third Space subjects' knowledge about the physical, spiritual, and/ or metaphysical is either shaped or shunned in educational spaces. Third Space Chicana Feminism offers new pedagogical approaches that recognize and empower Third Space bodies as subjects of knowledge, specifically those students residing in the borderlands. As a result, students' bodies can be read as texts and contributing sources of knowledge. By justifying the private, bodily space of the learner, Third Space Chicana Feminist theories allow for the democratic space of the classroom, thereby evoking pedagogical concepts including "theory in the flesh," "*nepantla*," and "*la facultad.*"

Anzaldúa's and Moraga's concept of "theory in the flesh" undergirds the theoretical method for understanding the political act of Third Space subjects' "flesh and blood experiences" (*This Bridge* 23). This concept supports a Chicana feminist saying that the personal is political and that our everyday life experiences significantly shape our epistemologies. This theoretical approach reclaims the bodily space of Third Space subjects, including their homes and communities—a significant gesture considering how history has written upon Third Space bodies. As a pedagogical approach, "a theory in the flesh" emphasizes how one's home knowledge contains ample cultural and cognitive resources with great potential use for classroom instruction.

Building from a theory of the body, Gloria Anzaldúa explores the spiritual and metaphysical dimensions of knowing the self. AnaLouise Keating points out that Anzaldúa's belief in the "interconnections among body, mind, and spirit" are key components in her theories; she further adds that, for Anzaldúa, spiritualty is a political process that is rooted in the body (8–9). Understanding how our identity is constructed and linked to the spiritual thus forms a significant part of Anzaldúa's theories (e.g., the concept of *nepantla* and *la facultad*).

In *Interviews/Entrevistas*, Anzaldúa proposes that the *mestiza* identity takes shape through a "process-in-the-making" where identity construction overlaps; she defines this overlap as *nepantla*, or a liminal space of the borderlands, and compares it to the process of birthing where you are in a womb state passing through the birth canal (239, 226). Pedagogically, the classroom can be seen as an extension of the birth canal Anzaldúa describes. Consider the opportunities for classrooms that embrace this concept; the space transforms itself into an almost maternal, caring space that houses opportunities for *nepantla*, where the subject develops what Anzaldúa defines as a state of *la facultad*.

Anzaldúa explains that *la facultad* is the capability to see and sense deeper realities (*Borderlands* 38). In her interviews, Anzaldúa relates it to a survival-like state that exists naturally in everyone, particularly in people of color. But then, she also contends that educational spaces expunge this mental state, often only privileging intellectual development and viewing emotional and/or spiritual development as tangential to academic matters (Rendón 3). It is through this mode of consciousness that one develops an empowered agency to better understand the world and a pedagogical strategy that encourages civic and social activism. Building from the pedagogical influences of Chicana Feminism, I now turn to the third and most identifiable concept of their scholarship: the construction of discursive practices that uniquely define Third Space realities.

THIRD SPACE CHICANA FEMINIST RHETORIC: "A RHETORIC OF DIFFERENCE"

Lisa A. Flores explains how Third Space Chicana Feminists can move beyond rhetorical borders with the creation of discursive spaces, or homes (143). By constructing a "rhetoric of difference," Chicana Feminists are able to develop their own unique identity and carve out their own spaces and places (143). By emphasizing Flores's notion of "a rhetoric of difference," I contend that Third Space Chicana Feminists articulate spatiality in a different way, as opposed to the other Third Space theorists discussed next.

Flores defines "a rhetoric of difference" as "repudiating mainstream discourse and espousing self- and group-created discourse" (145). By rejecting external discourses, Third Space subjects identify themselves as different from dominant culture and thus are able to establish self- and/ or group autonomy because they name themselves (145–146). Such is the case with the birth of the Third Space Chicana Feminist movement, which rejected US hegemonic feminist definitions and developed internal descriptions that better reflect the historical circumstances of the group and the nature of the oppression it faced (Flores 146). Third Space Chicana Feminism provides access to a different way of conceptualizing oppositional activity by articulating a "common speech" and "theoretical structure" that initially was denied or permitted by a hegemonic feminist theory (Flores 2).

Adela C. Licona considers alternative "spaces and places" that generate Third Space. She argues that, as a practice, Third Space reveals a differential consciousness that can engage creative forms of opposition to the limits of "dichotomous (mis)representations" (105). Third Space as a location allows for a space of shared understanding or meaning-making (105). Licona adds that a Third Space consciousness allows for dualities to be transcended, revealing reproductive spaces where subjects "put perspectives, lived experiences, and rhetorical performances into play" (105). Within Third Space sites, representational rhetorics emerge that Licona terms "(b)orderlands' rhetorics" (105).

Third Space consciousness that is inherent in *(b)orderlands' rhetoric* can be located in both academic and nonacademic discourses, ultimately positioning Third Space Chicana Feminists in what Anzaldúa would describe as a liminal space, or *nepantla*, where *la facultad* transforms all writing into a political act (105). As a result, Third Space complexities are placed on the periphery of academic borders and are considered to be "subversive" and "discursively disobedient" (106). To write *(b)orderlands* with the visible interruption of the parentheses is Licona's way of representing a "conscious transcendence to a generative Third Space of movement and messiness" (105). Third Space "movement" and "messiness" also allow its subjects to slip and slide across both sides of border[s] in order to unearth alternative ways of knowing and being (106). Thus, borrowing Licona's description of (b)orderlands rhetorics, with the interruption of parentheses, I contend that Third Space Chicana Feminists provide distinguishable theories, pedagogies, and discursive practices that articulate new modes of knowledge about the spatiality of the (b)orderlands—modes not entirely comprehended by other mainstream postmodern scholars.

Redefining Postmodern Interpretations of Third Space

Even though Edward Soja is commonly recognized as a key contributor to Third Space theories, his scholarship does not reflect a Third Space (b)orderland consciousness. For instance, his scholarship on the social consequences of spatiality and the elements that construct the spatiality of humans does not reflect and is not informed by the politics of the lived experiences of Third Space citizens. Instead, Soja extends the dialectic of spatial production based on the works of philosopher Henri Lefebvre.

Lefebvre defines space as a complex social construction, based on values and the production of meaning, which in turn shape spatial practices (e.g., knowledge). In *The Production of Space*, Lefebvre writes of modes of existence in social relationships to the extent that they have a spatial existence. If social relations project themselves into a space, they contribute to the production of space. Failing this, "the relations would remain in the realm of 'pure' abstraction...the realm of verbalism, verbiage and empty words" (129). In short, Lefebvre asserts that social relations only become authentic when they are "inscribed" in the production of space; without this collective process, the modes of existence are inauthentic (129). Like Lefebvre, Soja argues that space is a social process that extends beyond the geographical. He theorizes how the historical imagination of space contributes to the construction of "human geographies" and "geographical landscapes" (*Postmodern Geographies* 10–11).

In contrast, Pérez's emphasis on historical consciousness suggests that the social production of space occurs differentially, particularly for those who are occluded (e.g., Third Space citizens). The colonized represent a liminal identity within the decolonial imaginary; they are neither oppressed or oppressor but negotiate within the decolonial imaginary as *Othered* (7). Pérez points out how being denied or occluded a social existence at the boundaries of any given space does not prevent spatial existence but rather constructs existence in an alternative space, a perpetual in-between-space—a Third Space. It is here that silences are heard and become the negotiating spaces for the decolonizing subject, where Third Space agency is articulated (Pérez 5).

Pérez provides new modes of knowledge about the elements of Third Space. Unlike Soja, who defines Third Space as an "unimaginable universe…common to all of us yet never able to be completely seen and understood," Third Space Chicana Feminist theories are committed to creating a space where agency is enacted as a visible alternative to traditional notions of spatiality, whether "real" and/or "imagined" (Soja 56, 10).

Soja's interpretation of Third Space expands a theme embedded in Lefebvre's *The Production of Space* defined as "thirding-as-Othering" (Soja 60). The lure of binaries, according to Soja, introduces a third possibility whereby thirding-as-othering "introduces a critical 'other-than' choice that speaks and critiques through its otherness" (60). Thirding-as-othering provides an alternative reading about social space as a "thematic trialectic" or a "linked triad" where space is "perceived," "conceived," and "lived" (65). Yet, this trialectic returns to a spatial imagination that perpetually revolves around a dual mode of thinking about space: Firstspace, which is fixed on the materiality of spatial forms, and Secondspace, which is conceived ideas about space. Soja explains it is Firstspace that is often thought of as "real" and the Secondspace as "imagined" (10).

I agree with Soja that epistemologies "tend to privilege objectivity and materiality" and "become fixated on the material form of things in space: with human spatiality seen primarily as outcome or *product*" (75–76). Also, I understand why Soja accepts Secondspace epistemologies as distinguishable by their concentration on conceived rather than perceived knowledge about space. Soja argues that Secondspace is "entirely ideational, made up of projections into the empirical world from conceived or imagined geographies" (78–79). He points out how this common dualistic mindset about spatiality (i.e., Firstspace/Secondspace binaries) is limiting. Nonetheless, Soja's discussion of Third Space epistemologies as both "real-and-imagined," in which he proposes "everything comes together," is problematic in that he does not take into account the "unique diasporic configuration" that has shaped (b)orderland human geographies (Pérez xviii).

With limited knowledge about the real-and-imagined illusions of Third Space (b)orderlands, even Soja turns to postmodern spatial feminists who provide lived experiences of Third Space difference and identity. He indicates how a feminist critique of Third Space calls attention to the marginality and intersectionality of the psychological, social, and cultural borderlands of contemporary lived spaces (111). Even though Soja acknowledges how a privileged consciousness does not acknowledge the construction of Third Space human geographies, his discourse does not pronounce the realities of those Third Space citizens. Instead, Third Space Feminists' theories articulate the consciousness of marginalized individuals residing in proximity to real-and-imagined (b)orderland geographies.

For instance, Pérez defines this real-and-imagined intersectionality of Third Space as the "decolonial imaginary," or a tool to uncover interstitial spaces between real-and-imagined (or First- and Secondspace). She explains, that "by fusing the words 'decolonial' and 'imaginary,' each term riddled with meaning, I locate the decolonial within that which is intangible. Here the imaginary conjures fragmented identities, fragmented realities, that are 'real,' but a real that is in question" (6). Unlike Soja, Pérez challenges the historical divide between reality and *Other*ness by probing the discursive fields of history in a postmodern approach where all is imagined. She writes that historians have assigned regional labels that reflect spatial characteristics, yet masses continue to conceptualize history without challenging how discursive sites have been interpreted (4). It is within these interstitial spaces where the voices of the marginalized, ignored, or repressed are excavated and provided new platforms to enact oppositional consciousness (Bañuelos 97). As the subsequent section points out, it is through a (b)orderland consciousness that Third Space citizens put perspectives, lived experiences, and theoretical performances into play (Licona 105).

THIRD SPACE (B)ORDERLAND CONSCIOUSNESS

Anzaldúa exposed the multiple identities of Third Space (b)orderland subjects. She captured the ways literal, symbolic, and geographical spaces can hold multiple meanings as historical discursive sites. She paid attention to the physical, metaphysical, psychological, and spiritual interpretations of the borderland and how material and metaphoric borders are designed to define the places that are safe and unsafe (*Borderlands* 3). For Anzaldúa, the literal site of the US–Mexican border also represents a site of injustices and oppressions for the marginalized. Living within "*los intersticios*, the space between the different worlds she inhabits," is where (b)orderland subjects experience la facultad, the awareness "developed as a survival tactic that people, caught between two worlds, unknowingly cultivate" (*Borderlands* 39).

Anzaldúa further describes *los intersticios* as a transitional space of *nepantla*, which is Third Space consciousness of the (b)orderlands real-and-imagined. But more than this, it offers possibilities to be open to other perspectives with an acute sense of holistic awareness ("Now Let Us Shift" 544). Nepantla recontextualizes real-and-imagined geopolitical spaces, such as the (b)orderland, in order to redefine discursive archetypes and to recreate new theories that will rewrite the history of Third Space subjects (Anzaldúa, "Haciendo Caras/Making Face, Making Soul" xxv). Because the characteristics of (b)orderland human geographies are marked by a "unique diasporic configuration" influenced and shaped by discursive geographical and historical conflicts, a ubiquitous signifier of Chicanx literature is the transformation of these real-and-imagined Third Spaces (Pérez xviii).

Lisa Flores writes how the fight for space for Chicanx authors is partially driven by Soja's concept of Firstspace geographical influences. The Rio Grande, for example, serves as a physical (or "real") representation of the separation and isolation experienced by Mexican Americans living on the border (143). Although the US–Mexico border along the Rio Grande was set up (or "imagined") to define a sense of safety, in *Borderlands* Anzaldúa describes it as "*una herida abierta*," or an open wound where the "Third World grates against the first and bleeds" (3). The material manifestation of the borderlands, thus, represents a real-and-imagined site that positions Mexican Americans between two distinct worlds where "the sense of being neither truly Mexican nor truly American often results in feelings of isolation, where Chicanas/os may find that they do not belong in either land" (Flores 142–143). These feelings of tension and isolation result in a sense of urgency to struggle for a space and a home—prevalent themes of Chicanx literature.

Mary Pat Brady studies the urgency of understanding Third Space insights of Chicanx (b)orderland literature. She writes how a literary critique and spatial reading of it "offers an important theoretics of space, one that, like many critical space studies implicates the production of space in the everyday, in the social, but that unlike many space theories suggests the relevance of aesthetics, of 'the literary mode of knowing' for understanding the intermeshing of the spatial and the social." Brady points out how Chicanax (b)orderland literature offers "alternative methods of conceptualizing space...by refusing a too-rigid binary between the material and the discursive" (6).

For instance, Brady explains how the production of space also involves the processes that shape how places are understood, envisioned, defined, and experienced (7). Spaces shape sociality and are highly affective; places are felt and experienced (8). Because a notable theme of Chicanx (b)orderland literature is recognizing how Third Space relates to symbolic makers (e.g., home and family), the following section provides theoretical and pedagogical insight on how the epistemologies of the home and the community, spaces and places defined and studied by Chicana Feminists, are "highly affective" when shaping feelings and experiences.

SHAPING THIRD SPACE CHICANA FEMINIST EXPERIENCES

Luis C. Moll, Cathy Amanti, Deborah Neff, and Norma González study innovations in teaching that draw on the knowledge and skills found in local households of working Mexican Americans (132). They claim that educators should capitalize on the students' familiar spaces, such as their homes and communities, and they should organize classroom instruction that encourages students' "funds of knowledge," which they define as the culturally developed bodies of knowledge and skills essential for household or individual well-being (132–133). By tracing what is learned in the home, the authors point out how home-knowledge contains ample cultural and cognitive resources with great potential utility for classroom instruction (134). Funds of home-knowledge help equip students with strategies when confronted with challenges outside the home. For instance, the authors make clear how "household members" use their funds of knowledge in "dealing with changing, and often difficult, social and economic circumstances" (133). They point out their interest in how family members develop social networks as a means to establish meaningful relationships (133).

Investigating knowledge learned from home is not necessarily a new concept for Chicanx scholars. Dolores Delgado Bernal also studies how communication practices and learning that occur in the home and community—what she calls "pedagogies of the home"—often serve as a cultural knowledge base that helps Chicanx students negotiate daily experiences (113). Pedagogies of the home extend the dialectic of Chicana feminists by "putting cultural knowledge and language at the forefront to better understand lessons from the home space and local communities" (114).

Delgado Bernal implies that by drawing on the diverse linguistic and cultural resources of students' home spaces, educators can develop classroom spaces and assignments that are shaped by personal and collective experiences. This practice embraces Anzaldúa's and Moraga's theoretical concept of theory in the flesh, which articulates a Chicana Feminist insistence that the personal is political and that our everyday life experiences significantly shape our epistemologies. Much Chicanx (b)orderland literature embraces this theoretical perspective, articulating themes of racism, alienation, colonization, tragedy, or shame.

Edén Torres explains how these themes can be seen as Chicanxs' attempts to "grieve, to express the pain, and to heal … [but also] cause discomfort in people who try to deny that the damage exists" (13). Torres proposes how exposing a "lived theory" also allows Chicanx writers to "speculate on meaning, test our ideas, and articulate our objectives" as well as "to develop various methods for actualizing our desire for change" (3). One psychological method she recommends is the study of Post-Traumatic Stress Disorder (PTSD). Unlike conventional scholarship and existing theories that do little to address how people respond to emotional events, PTSD supplies Torres with an understanding of the shame-based behaviors that surface from critiquing "lived theory" (14).

Torres is quick to note how the manifestations of historic trauma and shame are not exclusive to Mexican Americans, nor does she insinuate that they are dysfunctional. Rather, she shows how this population has individually and/or collectively reacted to ongoing socioeconomic, political, and educational inequalities (16). She proposes that discovering meaning in our "lived theory" through analysis of PTSD experiences will reveal inherent survival abilities and the strength of our culture (16). Nonetheless, Torres also contends that lived theory extends beyond the individual to include the collective experiences of the community. She declares that the task of the authentic community is to "stop denying the effect on us as a people...and honor the struggle of others to become fully alive in a nation that so often despises us" (16). Torres claims that the collective historic trauma of racism, sexism, and classism has taken its toll on our communities, but as a culture we continue to overcome and reveal our ability to survive and resist oppression (18). Historic trauma plays a significant role in our ability to heal and/or continue destructive behaviors (18).

Torres's study of lived theory as it relates to trauma on the body reiterates the bodily significance of Third Space subjects. It also shows how those bodies construct real-and-imagined Third Space politics that extend to include the politics of the greater community and culture. Once we identify, explore, and heal from historic traumas, Torres claims, we are able to respond to those of others. Rather than be numb to the social, historical, political, and economic trauma that surrounds us, Torres's praxis of courage defines a notable pedagogical practice of Third Space Chicana Feminism, creating a space where the voices of the marginalized, ignored, or repressed are heard and empowered with a critical Third Space consciousness. Torres also highlights how Third Space Chicana Feminists invite us to confront issues that directly affect our bodies as a means for social and political transformation.

As a theory, Third Space Chicana Feminism provides a distinct platform, a Third Space, for marginalized identities to embody differential consciousness as a method to reinterpret and reimagine the world on their own terms and visions. As a pedagogy, Third Space Chicana Feminism introduces new methodologies and insights on educating marginalized bodies. As explored in this chapter, through its unique discourse practices, Third Space Chicana Feminism generates various ways of knowing marginalized identities and their experiences. It demonstrates the need for marginalized identities to occupy Third Space as a way to engage in the practices of differential consciousness that moves its citizens to notions of social justice. In doing so, we can begin to strategically re-envision how history has been written and how it can be re-envisioned in the space of the decolonial imaginary. Finally, the scholarship of Third Space Chicana

Feminists presents a mode of consciousness that collectively transforms hegemonic ideologies into their own revolutionary apparatus of love for enacting opposition social action in the postmodern world (Sandoval 146–7).

WORKS CITED

Anzaldúa, Gloria. *Borderlands/La Frontera: The New Mestiza.* 2nd ed. San Francisco: Spinsters/Aunt Lute, 1999. Print.

Anzaldúa, Gloria. *Interviews/Entrevistas*, ed. AnaLouise Keating. New York: Routledge, 2000. Print.

Anzaldúa, Gloria. Now Let Us Shift…The Path of Conocimiento…Inner Work, Public Acts. In *This Bridge We Call Home*, 540–576. New York: Routledge Press, 2002. Print.

Anzaldúa, Gloria, and Cherríe Moraga. *This Bridge Called My Back: Writings By Radical Women of Color.* 2nd ed. San Francisco: Kitchen Table Press, 1983. Print.

Bañuelos, Esthela L. Here They Go Again with the Race Stuff. In *Chicana/Latina Education in Everyday Life: Feminista Perspectives on Pedagogy and Epistemology*, eds. Dolores Delgado-Bernal, C. Alejandra Elenes, Francisca E. Godinez and Sofia Villenas, 95–112. Albany: SUNY P, 2006. Print.

Brady, Mary Pat. *Extinct Lands, Temporal Geographies: Chicana Literature and the Urgency of Space.* Durham: Duke University Press, 2002. Print.

Córdova, Teresa. The Emergent Writings of Twenty Years of Chicana Feminist Struggles: Roots and Resistance. In *The Handbook of Hispanic Cultures in the United States*, ed. Félix Padilla, 175–202. Houston: University of Houston, Arte Público Press.

Flores, Lisa A. Creating Discursive Space Through a Rhetoric of Difference. *Quarterly Journal of Speech* 82, no. 2 (1996): 142. *Communication & Mass Media Complete.*

Jameson, Frederic. *Postmodernism, or, The Cultural Logic of Late Capitalism.* Durham, NC: Duke University Press, 1991. Print.

Keating, AnaLouise. Introduction. *The Gloria Anzaldúa Reader*, ed. AnaLouise Keating, 1–15. Durham: Duke University Press, 2009. Print.

Lefebvre, Henri. *The Production of Space.* Oxford, UK and Cambridge, MA: Blackwell, 1991. Print.

Licona, Adela C. (B)orderlands' Rhetoric and Representations: The Transformative Potential of Feminist Third Space Scholarship and Zines. *National Women's Studies Association Journal* 17 (2005b): 104–129.

Licona, Adela C. *Third Space Site, Subjectivities and Discourses: Reimagining the Representational Potentials of (B)orderlads' Rhetorics.* Dissertation. Iowa State University, 2005a. Ames, Iowa. UMI, 2006. Print.

Pérez, Emma. *The Decolonial Imaginary*. Bloomington: Indiana University Press, 1999. Print.

Saldívar-Hull, Sonia. *Feminism on the Border: Chicana Gender Politics and Literature*. Berkley: University of California Press, 2000. Print.

Sandoval, Chela. *Methodology of the Oppressed*. Minneapolis: University of Minnesota Press, 1991. Print.

Soja, Edward W. *Third Space: Journeys to Los Angeles and Other Real-and-Imagined Places*. Oxford: Blackwell Publishing, 1996. Print.

PART IV

Political Rhetoric

CHAPTER 11

Illegal

Amanda Espinosa-Aguilar

Throughout the 1980s and 1990s, right-wing politicians, along with organizations, such as U.S. English, came close to having English declared the official language of the United States. For many people, this would have resulted in limited and unequal access to education, healthcare, legal aid, and other services. The politicians and organizations used rhetorics of fear to convince Anglos—and some people of color—that multilingual Americans threaten the nation's stability. Now, these same groups have turned their attention to an even more contested topic: immigration. Discussions about immigration into the United States often use hyperbolic language that reflects and reinforces an us-versus-them mentality. It is a language of exclusion that has gained prominence in a proliferation of state and federal anti-immigration legislation that seeks to blame, exploit, and dehumanize immigrants.

This chapter examines how two key terms, *immigrant* and *citizen*, are used in these measures to raise unsubstantiated fears in the minds of voters. Often, the fears are tied to the distribution of limited resources. John Luque notes that "the proponents for immigration enforcement laws argue that United States taxpayer dollars are unfairly spent on unauthorized immigrants who place a burden on public schools, hospitals, courts and

A. Espinosa-Aguilar (✉)
Department of English, Columbia Basin College, Pasco, WA, USA

© The Editor(s) (if applicable) and The Author(s) 2016   155
I.D. Ruiz, R. Sánchez (eds.), *Decolonizing Rhetoric and
Composition Studies*, DOI 10.1057/978-1-137-52724-0_11

jails, and depress wages" (31). Unfortunately, such rhetorics of fear help perpetuate a cycle of disenfranchisement for many American people of color. In response to this proliferation of anti-immigrant discourse, those of us who teach rhetoric can train our students in critical discourse analysis, which examines the constitutive role that language plays in the shaping of such dehumanizing policies.

Parsing the Terms: Citizen and Immigrant...and Everything in Between

Although many in the United States imagine it to be a land of immigrants coexisting in postracial harmony, in modern usage, the term *immigrant* is often associated with danger. According to anthropologist Claudia Strauss:

> There are narrow and broad ways of understanding immigrants as security threats. The narrow sense is a traditional interpretation of security threats as military and policing issues (e.g., immigrants as potential terrorists and criminals). The broader sense ... brings together under the umbrella of "security" a variety of ways immigrants can be represented as threats: not only as terrorists, criminals, and unauthorized entrants but also as overwhelming the welfare state and challenging the cultural basis of national identity. (265)

Today's immigrant, then, is often seen by native-born Anglos and racial minorities alike as an outsider who abuses the social welfare system, the economic system, and the criminal justice system. For instance, the Pew Research Center for Hispanic Trends has found that "Native-born Latinos are significantly less likely than the foreign born to see immigrants as a strength (69 % versus 85 %) and are almost three times as likely to say new arrivals are a burden (20 % versus 7 %)" (Lopez et al. 1).

Immigration has become a hot topic for candidates running for any office, from city council to president. As a result, how the media and politicians and their donors use the words *citizen* and *immigrant* often reveals their attitudes on this issue. In today's political climate, these words are understood as opposites: the first implying a native-born person, the second meaning an alien. However, there is instead a continuum of immigrants, separable into categories, as indicated in Fig. 11.1. If we examine each of these categories, we can describe their respective levels of privilege.

Citizen	Documented	Undocumented or Unauthorized	Illegal
(White) privileged under threat	Status preservationist	Usually not White	Person of color
Native born and White	Resident alien holding Green card or Visa	Insufficient Documentation	Non-native no documents
Legal / law abiding	Skilled / law abiding	Mostly law abiding	Criminals who abuse the system
Multi-generational	Multi-generational	Multi-generational	1st gen. aliens

Fig. 11.1 Variations on types of immigrants in US society

Citizen Immigrants

Not all immigrants are created equal. The far left column in the figure shows the characteristics of those immigrants who have been members of the United States for so long that they and their offspring think of themselves as "native"-born. These are the "us" in the us-versus-them rhetoric of anti-immigration groups; they may feel a "threat" from recent immigrants. Such threats include loss of privilege, increased tax burden, and rising crime.

These nativists fear losing the status and privilege they feel they have earned. The idea is that as others try to enter the middle class, someone has to leave to make room for them. Consequently, they see immigrants as a drain on public coffers, as a burden on welfare programs, and as abusers of social services. On talk radio, televised news, or in print journalism, taxpayer burden is most commonly used to justify the passage of anti-immigration legislation. As John Luque notes: "[M]edia argument framing and public discourse present a biased account of the unfair burden on United States taxpayers from unauthorized immigrants using taxpayer-subsidized medical and social services" (41).

In states with depleted budgets, anti-immigration laws are often valued and passed because they are presented as a way to decrease the alleged tax burden from which most states' legal citizens want relief. In *Language Loyalties*, Carol Schmid notes that "during periods of high immigration, economic restructuring, and recession … the notion of status preservation [makes] declining groups seek to maintain their eroding position by identifying with extremist causes" (203). This may explain why so many Americans endorse and elect candidates opposed to immigration.

Documented Immigrants (Foreign Nationals/Qualified Aliens)

Although this term is not as positive as citizen, documented immigrants still receive positive reactions to their immigration status in the United States because they often are perceived as giving more to society than they are taking from it. This category applies to researchers, scholars, inventors, entertainers, and the like who hold Green Cards or visas usually obtained with the help of major organizations, politicians, CEOs, and/or colleges. People of color in this group often practice color-on-color racism or inter-racial racism.

Undocumented or Unauthorized Immigrants

Undocumented or *Unauthorized*, terms in the third column in Fig. 11.1, imply fewer positive connotations than the previous one. Of the two terms, some claim that the latter is the more pejorative because it suggests something having been done without permission. In fact, at least 11 million people currently live in the United States without legal authorization to do so (Passel and Cohn 2010, 2011). However, only the non-White undocumented immigrant seems to experience backlash. A study conducted by the Center for Urban Economic Development at the University of Illinois at Chicago found that "race is an important dimension of the exploitation of undocumented Latino workers" (Mehta et al. 2002). This reality simply highlights the racist undertones of the immigration debate, where undocumented white Europeans are embraced by society, and Latinxs are criminalized, detained, deported, and/or shunned.

ILLEGAL (ALIEN) IMMIGRANTS

The term in the far right column, *illegal*, is of course the most derogatory, lending itself to acts of racism more easily than the rest. In addition, referring to immigrants as illegal *aliens* (a common term) literally dehumanizes them. The National Association of Hispanic Journalists has denounced "the use of the degrading terms 'alien' and 'illegal alien' to describe undocumented immigrants because it casts them as adverse, strange beings, inhuman outsiders who come to the U.S. with questionable motivations" (Rubio 2).

As noted in Fig. 11.1, those named as illegal aliens are often people of color, are often the first of their family to immigrate to the United States, and reflexively are considered criminals and abusers of American social programs. Gomberg-Munoz further argues that US immigration policies "have been legitimized by a rhetoric of criminality that stigmatizes Latino immigrant workers and intensifies their exploitation" (339).

For hate groups, using such rhetoric is effective because it is easier to deny rights and humanity to an alien than it is to a person. In addition, references to criminality are justified because these immigrants broke the law simply by coming to the US. Well-organized hate groups embrace the terms *illegal* and *alien* to solidify differences between "native" citizens and others. The irony is that, although they fear such groups' alleged criminality, the anti-immigration legislation they endorse creates an environment in which immigrants are arrested and their criminal records are expanded. Thus begins a self-fulfilling prophecy of life-long recidivism. In a strange twist, a number of media outlets, including National Public Radio, have noted that large for-profit prisons, such as the Corrections Corporation of America, applaud anti-immigration laws because they provide them with the resource they most need in order to grow: prisoners (Luque et al. 41).

As debates about immigration increasingly appear during election campaigns, so will anti-immigrant legislation and related anti-Latinx rhetoric. The only way to a constructive discussion about immigration, and to a solution for the problem, is through a massive restructuring of our thinking, particularly the language we use to label the people involved. The next section discusses the current political landscape by looking at those who subscribe to and promote these dehumanizing ways of defining immigrants within state and federal legislation.

PARSING RHETORICS OF FEAR IN ELECTION MATERIALS AND LEGISLATION

At the federal and state levels, legislation has been, or is being, enacted containing language that reinforces *linguicism*, which Tove Skutnabb-Kangas and Robert Phillipson define as "ideologies, structures, and practices which are used to legitimate, effectuate, and reproduce an unequal division of power and resources (both material and immaterial) between groups which are defined on the basis of language" (quoted in Phillipson 47). An examination of materials sent to voters, as well as three pieces of existing legislation, demonstrates that anti-immigrant rhetoric is not limited to media coverage and hardline nativists.

Linguicism in Ballots and Election Materials

For more than two decades, organizations such as U.S. English have promoted the idea that immigrants unfairly receive special treatment, particularly in the form of bilingual ballots that valid citizens would never need. On the U.S. English website, chairman and CEO Mauro E. Mujica writes:

> Under our Constitution, only American citizens can vote. According to the Immigration and Naturalization Service, applicants for citizenship must demonstrate "an ability to read, write and speak...simple words and phrases...in our common language, English. [Lack of English] will leave them blindly picking at straws since the majority of "campaigning" by politicians will be done in English. Moreover, multilingual ballots throw open the doors to coercion, fraud, and in the absence of illegality, mistakes. How do we know that the "translators"—who in all likelihood have their own political biases—will translate materials properly and fairly?

Mujica's language is intended to scare and anger nativist voters. It implies that immigrants do not want to assimilate, as evidenced by their need for multilingual ballots. It claims those who do not understand English will cast a ballot ignorant (i.e., lacking knowledge) of the candidates and the issues. It suggests that immigrants should not be allowed to vote if they do not understand English because election fraud will result.

Other examples of linguicism appear in campaign documents sent by the parties hoping to elect certain candidates. All registered voters have seen them; they fill mailboxes or are left as door hangers advertising a candidate's views on the pressing issues of the day. During the midterm elections of 2014, immigration played a role in the platforms of many of the candidates seeking national office. This was especially true in the state of Washington, where George Cicotte ran for the state's Fourth Congressional District seat. Because the voters in the district are mostly US-born citizens, it comes as no surprise that his election materials used rhetorics of fear when discussing immigrants. For example, an advertisement titled "Introducing George Cicotte's Contract with Eastern Washington: A Bold and Conservative Commitment for Our Future" contains a list of actions he would take if elected; one proposed the creation of an American Immigration Reform Act. This act's stated intention was to "defend our nation," "enforce stiff provisions for immediate deportation of all who enter our country illegally to commit crime, or to take advantage of our social safety net," and to create a "visa system for immigrants who can demonstrate the ability to make positive contributions to our US economy and who can avoid all criminal actions."

Note how this language recalls that of anti-immigration interests who routinely use us-versus-them keywords such as "unity" and "our." Such groups influence voters and garner favor from politicians by couching their views in politically correct language so as to not appear racist. For example, on its website, NumbersUSA claims that "race and ethnicity should play no role in the debate and establishment of immigration policy." On the surface, who wouldn't support such a sentiment? However, this masks the fact that the group actually wants to prevent almost all immigration to the United States.

The site states: "We favor reductions in immigration numbers toward traditional levels that would allow present and future generations of Americans to enjoy a stabilizing U.S. population and a high degree of individual liberty, mobility, environmental quality, worker fairness and fiscal responsibility." This sounds innocuous, but further examination reveals a decidedly anti-immigrant stance. How will reduction in numbers take place? That is, through the elimination of "extended-family 'chain migration,' [t]he visa lottery, [and] employment-based visas for foreign workers of non-extraordinary skills."

In the United States, language minorities and immigrants are often disenfranchised, yet they are often bamboozled into voting for candidates who suggest that achieving the American dream-myth implicitly requires them to support legislators who actually can hurt them. Therefore, many follow the nativist idea of assimilation that, according to Joseph Leibowicz, "[rejects] the contention that one [can] keep one's mother tongue, yet still be a good citizen of the United States." According to this view, "learning English [is] not enough—committed immigrants [have] to cast off their alien tongues along with their alien status" (Leibowicz 105).

Along with the growth of the anti-immigrant groups and the draconian laws they have helped to pass, there has been a rise in anti-immigrant rhetoric. The message from the ironically named Federation for American Immigration Reform (FAIR) and the Center for Immigration Studies (CIS), as well as NumbersUSA, is one of intolerance, promoting a highly charged racial discourse, which provides ammunition to media conglomerates that capitalize on the negative narrative of immigration.

Linguicism in Legislation: H.R. 240 and H. Con. Res 28

Hate groups are some of the best funded and influential special interests affecting American politics today. According to *The New York Times*, NumbersUSA, U.S. English, FAIR, and CIS "were influential in the congressional defeat of the Dream Act in 2010, and the drafting of Arizona's notorious SB 1070" (quoted in Rubio 1). They also served as the foundation for Georgia's HB 87—the "Illegal Immigration Reform and Enforcement Act of 2011"—that restricts access to programs that are not federally mandated to only those who can verify that they are lawful US citizens. In addition, these entities were players in two federal acts related to immigration. One is H.R. 240, or the Department of Homeland Security Appropriations Act of 2015, which President Obama signed into law on March 3 and which included his November 2014 amnesty for undocumented immigrants. Of course, citizens who fear losing their relatively privileged status see such amnesties as illegal and unconstitutional.

Less than two weeks after the passage of H.R. 240, House Concurrent Resolution 28 was submitted to Congress containing rhetoric suggesting a purposeful use of exclusionary, anti-immigrant language. Notably, it states:

> Whereas Article I, Sect. 8 of the Constitution of the United States gives Congress the power "to establish a uniform rule of naturalization"; Whereas only Congress has the constitutional authority to legislate which classes of aliens may be granted legal status and work authorization; and Whereas the passage of H.R. 240 to fund the Department of Homeland Security and protect against ongoing terrorist threats could be misconstrued as the consent of Congress to the President's illegal and unconstitutional executive amnesty: Now, therefore, be it Resolved by the House of Representatives (the Senate concurring), That Congress affirms that the actions taken by the President to implement executive amnesty exceed his constitutional authority, and thus are unlawful.

Through their choice of words, the authors' intent was to present the President in the worst possible light, and themselves as victims.

The Resolution starts by bemoaning their loss of power to choose who may immigrate legally, and to establish immigration policy for the country. It then employs a scare tactic by equating unauthorized migration with terrorism and implied rising crime rates. Finally, it deploys us-versus-them rhetoric by stating that the desire to protect the nation from terrorists by funding the DHS could be construed as supporting the illegal and excessive actions of one man, namely President Obama. Such rhetoric of fear, then, permeates not just the national debate on immigration but the actual laws being enacted because of it. Those who see themselves as citizens seem to believe that they have much to lose by favoring humane immigration laws.

Georgia's House Bill 87

Unlike the legislation dealing with federal immigration policy, Georgia's HB 87 amended multiple chapters of the Official Code of Georgia that pertain to immigration. Entitled the "Illegal Immigration Reform and Enforcement Act of 2011," by far the most common argument of the bill's proponents was the cost of unauthorized immigrants to Georgia's taxpayers because of burdens on the state's institutions for providing education, healthcare, and criminal justice services. This argument was especially salient in light of the economic downturn the state was experiencing. While opponents of the bill labeled it as "papers please" or "Juan Crow" legislation, its supporters rallied around the catchphrase, "What part of 'illegal' don't you understand?" (quoted in Luque 35). The supporters argued that undocumented immigrants are breaking the law, and federal law needs to be enforced by the states because the federal government has not enacted comprehensive immigration reform or adequately protected the US–Mexico border.

Passage of HB 87 has had wide-ranging consequences. It is now a felony punishable by jail time and/or a fine for any person, native-born or not, to willingly help, transport, or employ anyone deemed to be an "illegal alien" (a term that appears throughout the text). Mandatory use of the E-Verify program by employers also is required under HB 87. But most disturbing are the parts related to its "Secure and Verifiable Identity Act" in Sections 8 and 9. Based on Arizona's SB 1070, the law states: "When attempting to determine the immigrant status of a suspect…a peace officer shall be authorized to use any reasonable means available to determine the immigration status of the suspect."

Although HB 87 tries to avoid racial profiling by stating that "a peace officer shall not consider race, color, or national origin in implementing the requirements of this Code," it seems absurd to believe that, for example, a young, white woman would ever be asked to verify her immigration status to an officer in Georgia. The same section gives officers "the power to arrest, with probable cause, any person suspected of being an illegal alien." The obvious question, then, is: In the absence of racial profiling for markers such as color and bilingualism, how would an officer determine probable cause? Moreover, Section 9 provides officers who enforce the law "immunity from damages or liability from such actions."

Even more alarming, however, is Section 11 of HB 87, which creates (subject to available funding) an incentive program for enforcing the law: "In awarding such grants or incentives, the council shall be authorized to consider and give priority to local areas with the highest crime rates for crimes committed by illegal aliens." Because Georgia has witnessed a "96 percent increase in the proportion of Hispanics in the state since 2000; [and] they now comprise approximately 850,000 people or 8.8 percent of Georgia's total population" (US Census Bureau 2012), it seems obvious which communities will be targeted to earn those incentives.

Ironically, groups representing Georgia's agricultural community overwhelmingly opposed the bill and estimated that as much as $1 billion a year would be lost (Luque et al. 32). In 2012, many farmers left their crops unpicked for lack of workers. Although undocumented immigrants are now considered criminals in Georgia, and thus unemployable under this law, Governor Nathan Deal (2011–) had the audacity to propose using convicted criminals on probation to work on Georgia farms during harvest. According to Luque et al., Georgia farmers prefer "continued access to a disenfranchised, low-skilled, easily replaceable immigrant labor pool." Moreover, they note that "labor trends have shown that United States citizens are either incapable or unwilling to take many low-skilled jobs vacated by low-wage immigrant laborers (e.g., farmworkers, poultry processing workers)" (32).

Even a cursory analysis of these laws shows that linguicism is very much a part of the crafting of anti-immigration legislation. Rhetorics of fear lead to the passage of laws that are inherently racist and are responsible for the continued disenfranchisement of all immigrants, especially Latinxs. But border militarization and anti-immigrant policies have not reduced the flow of labor migration; they have merely "illegalized" it, thereby further legitimizing the exploitation of immigrant workers.

ULTIMATE EFFECTS OF THE ANTI-IMMIGRANT RHETORICS OF FEAR

Immigration is, of course, nothing new to America; however, what matters is how we talk about it and what we do about it. In 1965, the Hart-Cellar Act "equalized the national origins quota system and subjected transmigrants from Mexico and other Latin American countries to numerical restrictions for the first time ever" (Gomberg-Munoz 342). The inevitable result of this legislation was an increase in unauthorized immigration that continues into 2016. The assignment of criminal status to a broad segment of the non-White population is a double-edged sword that at once reinforces existing inequality and legitimizes it with rhetorics of fear. As Claudia Strauss has noted: "[S]killful politicians can creatively combine conventional discourses with rhetorical strategies of concession, springboarding, and co-optation to align with multiple constituencies, including ones on opposing sides of an issue" (262).

Scholars of rhetorical studies need to do more to teach all students to recognize these manipulative political rhetorical gestures. As David Livingston Smith notes:

> The study of dehumanization needs to be made a priority. Universities, governments, and nongovernmental organizations need to put money, time, and talent into figuring out exactly how dehumanization works and what can be done to prevent it. Maybe then we can use this knowledge to build a future that is less hideous than our past: a future with no Rwandas, no Hiroshimas, and no Final Solutions. (273)

Recognizing the dehumanizing strategies of anti-immigrant groups, candidates, media, and legislation is a first step toward draining their powers.

Another—perhaps more important—step is teaching voters to resist the language of dehumanization. The terms *citizen* and *immigrant* may never disappear from our language, nor will debates about this topic. The best we may hope for is to naturalize the terms, but without modifiers; that is, no more use of adjectives such as illegal, documented, naturalized, native-born, privileged, legal, or alien. It should be just as distasteful to use these terms—these dehumanizing tactics—as it is to use any of the ethnic and racial slurs that no longer have a place in respectful discourse. In its campaign to "Drop the I-Word," Colorline.com states that "no human being is illegal." Perhaps, by pressuring politicians to stop using such language, and by boycotting officials and groups who continue to endorse legislation that codifying its use, we can help put an end to dehumanization.

WORKS CITED

Cicotte for Congress. Introducing George Cicotte's Contract with Eastern Washington: A Bold and Conservative Commitment for Our Future. Advertisement. 2014, July 14. Print.

Golash-Boza, Tanya. *Immigration Nation: Raids, Detentions, and Deportations in Post-9/11 America.* Boulder, CO: Paradigm Publishers, 2012. Print.

Gomberg-Muñoz, Ruth. Inequality in a 'Postracial' Era: Race, Immigration and Criminalization of Low-Wage Labor. *Du Bois Review* 9 (2012): 339–353. ProQuest. Web. April 20, 2015.

H.Con.Res.28 — 114th Congress (2015–2016). 2015. Expressing the Sense of Congress that the President's Executive Amnesty is Illegal Notwithstanding Passage of H.R. 240, the Department of Homeland Security Appropriations Act of 2015. March 23. Web. January 15, 2015.

H.R. 240 — 114th Congress (2015–2016). Department of Homeland Security Appropriations Act of 2015, 6 January. Web. January 15, 2015.

HB 87. 2011. Illegal Immigration Reform and Enforcement Act of 2011. July 10, 2011. Web. <http://www.legis.ga.gov/Legislation/20112012/116631.pdf>. January 10, 2013.

Leibowicz, Joseph. Official English: Another Americanization Campaign? In *Language Loyalties*, ed. James Crawford, 101–111. Chicago: U of Chicago P, 1992. Print.

Lopez, Mark, Rich Morin, and Paul Taylor. Illegal Immigration Backlash Worries, Divides Latinos October 28, 2010. <http://www.pewhispanic.org/files/reports/128.pdf>. December 10, 2014. Web.

Luque, John S., Angel Bowers, Ahmed Kabore, and Ric Stewart. Who Will Pick Georgia's Vidalia Onions? A Text-Driven Content Analysis of Newspaper Coverage on Georgia's 2011 Immigration Law. *Human Organization* 72 (2013): 31–43. ProQuest. Web. April 20, 2015.

Mehta, Chirag, Nik Theodore, Iliana Mora, and Jennifer Wade. Chicago's Undocumented Immigrants: An Analysis of Wages, Working Conditions, and Economic Contributions. UIC Center for Urban Economic Development. 2009, July 20. <http://www.urbaneconomy.org/node/52> Web. September 28, 2014.

Mujica, Mauro E. Bilingual Ballots Are UnAmerican. U.S. English.com, 2002, July 31. Web. January 1, 2015. <http://www.us-english.org/view/54>.

Numbersusa.com/about. n.d. Web. April 5, 2015.

Nunez, D. Carolina. War of the Words: Aliens, Immigrants, Citizens, and the Language of Exclusion. *Brigham Young University Law Review* 2013, no. 6 (2013): 1517–1562. ProQuest. Web. April 20, 2015.

Passel, Jeffrey, and D'Vera Cohn. A Portrait of Unauthorized Immigration in the United States. *Pew Research Center's Hispanic Trends.* 2009, April 14. <http://pewhispanic.org/files/reports/107.pdf> Web. August 13, 2014.

Passel, Jeffrey, and D'Vera Cohn. Unauthorized Immigrant Population: National and State Trends, 2010. *Pew Research Center's Hispanic Trends.* 2011, February 1. <http://pewhispanic.org/reports/report.php?ReportID=133> Web. May 27, 2014.

Passel, Jeffrey, and D'Vera Cohn. U.S. Unauthorized Immigration Flows Are Down Sharply Since Mid-Decade. *pewhispanic.org.* September 10, 2010. <http://www.pewhispanic.org/files/reports/126.pdf> Web. November 1, 2014.

Phillipson, Robert. *Linguistic Imperialism.* Oxford: Oxford UP, 1992. Print.

Rubio, Angelica. Undocumented, Not Illegal: Beyond the Rhetoric of Immigration Coverage. *NACLA Report on the Americas* 44, no. 6 (2011): 50–52. ProQuest. Web. April 20, 2014.

Schmid, Carol. The English Only Movement: Social Bases of Support and Opposition Among Anglos and Latinos. *Language Loyalties,* ed. James Crawford, 202–209. Chicago: U of Chicago P, 1992. Print.

Smith, David Livingstone. *Less Than Human: Why We Demean, Enslave, and Exterminate Others.* New York: St. Martin's Press, 2011. Print.

Strauss, Claudia. How Are Language Constructions Constitutive? Strategic Uses of Conventional Discourses About Immigration. *Journal of International Relations and Development* 16, no. 2 (2013): 262–293. ProQuest. Web. April 20, 2014.

United States Census Bureau. 2012. Georgia QuickFacts from the US Census. <http.7/ quickfacts.census.gov/qfd/states/ 1 3000.html> March 26, 2012. Web.

CHAPTER 12

Mojado

Marcos del Hierro

To be called a mojado is to be delegitimized for transgressing boundaries. The word is a mark of shame signifying that you feel your homeland is not good enough to provide what you and your family need. But mojados assert agency in the face of multivalent resistance. If they succeed, then they can provide for their families or themselves. If they fail, they risk humiliation, judgment, and even death. Ultimately, to be a mojado is an act of humility—you put your head down and struggle.

This chapter defines *mojado* as a term that simultaneously signifies the politics of legitimacy, citizenship, and belonging for Latinxs and the hustle required to succeed in spite of a system built on colonialism and white supremacy. In recognizing that words and their definitions can change according to context, it first examines how borders are physically, legally, and psychologically constructed to determine who may claim legitimacy in the United States. Latinxs, in spite of legal status, often face discrimination, which renders us all mojados in some aspect. As a response, Latinxs must get moving in order to survive and succeed. Finally, the chapter focuses on Latinxs in academia as an example of how many teachers,

M. del Hierro (✉)
Department of English, University of New Hampshire, Durham, NH, USA

© The Editor(s) (if applicable) and The Author(s) 2016   169
I.D. Ruiz, R. Sánchez (eds.), *Decolonizing Rhetoric and Composition Studies*, DOI 10.1057/978-1-137-52724-0_12

students, administrators, and staff must live with the daily reminder that they are not considered legitimate bodies within the United States.

According to Enrique G. Murillo, the term *mojado* is used to construct undocumented migrants as "newcomers" to the United States who cross "…in clandestine fashion; taking their chances with others in crossing the border to rejoin their families, make emergency visits, take up waiting employment on the other side, escape the poverty (or all these things)" (18–19). Identifying migrants as newcomers presumes that they have no ties to, contact with, or familiarity of the United States. This is a particularly sinister distinction in that it ignores the movement of people, communities, and borders throughout the history of the Americas.

The label mojado—which literally means *wet*—is often used to conflate multiple subjectivities. First, not all immigrants cross bodies of water to reach the United States. Second, not all undocumented people are actually immigrants. Some children are born to undocumented immigrants and are never officially reported to the government. Third, mojados are often assumed to be only Mexican, which ignores those coming from Central and South America who must cross several national borders. These distinctions argue for a definition of mojado that pays attention to the complexities that make up identities and labels.

A Chicano student confided in me that he cared deeply about the immigration debate because his mother was undocumented, but born in the United States. The mother was born in a migrant camp and grew up without papers. She should have all the rights of a legal citizen but lives in fear that she may be deported to Mexico if ever asked to prove her citizenship.

One of the dangers of conflating mojados is that it conflates danger itself; Murillo describes the perils:

> Border-crossers are often referred to as *pollos*, or chickens, because like chickens that may end up plucked and eaten, they are equally as vulnerable of what awaits in-between and on *el otro lado* (the other side). Entering the United States via holes in rusting fences, rat-infested tunnels, confined spaces of car trunks, flooding rivers, train cars, or darting across freeways, and then walking on back trails in mountain and desert areas, sometimes days on end without food or water, is a life-threatening journey. (19)

Murillo also mentions thieves who pillage and murder crossers, as well as Immigration and Naturalization Service (INS) and Homeland Security agents who are waiting on the other side to detain, abuse, and possibly kill. If that is not enough, those who survive must be constantly vigilant while working for employers who have the power to exploit their legal status.

Murillo writes that "mojados often must then live in concealment, changing their names, identities, and sometimes nationalities, forced to buy and carry fake birth certificates, false declarations of citizenship, micas chuecas (falsified greencards) and use social security numbers that belong to others" (19). Opportunists exist on all sides for those waiting to prey upon unsuspecting and desperate migrants. It is a constant test of physical, mental, and emotional strength. It often involves failure and death.

Surviving as a mojado means engaging with a set of rhetorics. The slang produced by this system signals the power dynamics in play, which heavily favor coyotes, *La Migra*, and other kinds of *rateros* (thieves). Those who choose to cross must understand what it means to be a *pollito* and the vulnerability they are understood and presumed to have. This vulnerability includes the expectation that failure is the most desirable outcome for all involved, except for migrants making the journey. Mojados also must understand the power of symbols, especially of objects, such as Green Cards, birth certificates, and social security cards, that will grant legitimacy and entrance into opportunities for work. Along with knowledge of these symbols, mojados must have the rhetorical knowledge necessary to navigate institutions in the United States that grant access to jobs, housing, and so on. This juggling act of danger, documents, and identities makes being a mojado extremely difficult. The structures that govern the stakes for all participants are borders, which are informed by colonialism, racism, and white supremacy.

Murillo adds a second, theoretical or metaphorical dimension to the term *mojado*. He argues that the marginalization of Mexicans and Chicanxs extends beyond that of undocumented migrants. He recognizes the danger of extending the term this way: it risks appropriating the struggle and suffering of a less privileged group in order to romanticize the struggles and suffering of relatively more privileged group. But because of the insights that may result, he believes the risk is worth taking:

> Though I don't have a reason in my current life-situation to cross the Rio Grande, the phenomenon is all too familiar to me having been raised along the United States/Mexican *Frontera* (borderlands) (*sic*), and I choose to

use the real-life metaphor as an experiential and culturally-genealogical tool to make meaning of my cultural, racial, ethnic, discursive, political, theoretical, and even class crossings into ethnography and academia. (19)

Murillo locates his credibility in living, witnessing, and experiencing the "noticeable economic and lifestyle disparity between both sides of the border" (19). He remembers noticing at a young age the ways US tourists flaunted their wealth while haggling with poor Mexican merchants. His community was socialized to understand the power differences between nations, people, and citizenship status.

DEFINING BORDERS

If you grew up anywhere near the Ciudad Juarez-El Paso border, you see that the Rio Grande was literally turned into an artificial boundary when concrete was laid down in order to firmly set the river's place. Our grandparents remember when the river was natural and how it started shifting and favoring the Mexican side. The United States insisted on laying down concrete because it did not want to lose any of the land it rightfully stole during the Treaty of Guadalupe-Hidalgo.

The fight for economic, political, and social power produces the danger that exists for mojados. The Mexico-U.S. border establishes and maintains these conditions. Gloria Anzaldúa theorizes the border as "*una herida abierta* where the Third World grates against the first and bleeds. And before a scab forms it hemorrhages again, the lifeblood of two worlds merging to form a third country—a border culture" (25). For her, the Mexico-US border produces something new constantly, and that act is a painful one. It never quite heals, and it never quite dies, but it always continues. There is the desire to unite, which is produced by the people and communities that see the border as an artificial boundary imposed on their homelands, the wildlife that doesn't understand how the borders work, and the weather that doesn't care that there are borders. Then there is the desire to separate, which is artificially drawn by the US and Mexican governments, imposed by constructing walls and canals, and defended by militarized guards.

Understanding how borders function, particularly between the United States and Mexico, is important because it helps us understand how what happens on the border is deliberate. Anzaldúa theorizes that borders are constructed to divide and classify people. Those who live on a border do

not fall neatly on one side or another, which marks them as *atravesados.*
She writes:

> Gringos in the U.S. Southwest consider the inhabitants of the borderlands
> transgressors, aliens—whether they possess documents or not, whether
> they're Chicanos, Indians or Blacks. Do not enter, trespassers will be raped,
> maimed, strangled, gassed, shot. The only "legitimate" inhabitants are those
> in power, the whites and those who align themselves with whites. Tension
> grips the inhabitants of the borderlands like a virus. Ambivalence and unrest
> reside there and death is no stranger. (25–26)

Part of understanding how borders function, within the context of
the United States, is realizing that they are informed by colonialism and
systemic white supremacy. To maintain the legitimacy of the border, the
United States constructs a demarcation that extends from land to people.
Anzaldúa points out that those who happen to call the area on and near
the border home are turned into outsiders and are considered threats to
establishing difference. Nonnormative bodies and subjectivities complicate identities, allegiances, and communities. In other words, the United
States needs a stark contrast to exist between itself and Mexico, which
means establishing normative identities, language, attitudes, and so forth.
Because it is a white settler colonial military occupation on Native Lands,
the United States chooses whiteness, the English language, and a superior
attitude over Mexico.

One way to understand how borders and debates over immigration
are tied to colonialism and white supremacy is to reverse the roles of who
belongs and who is the outsider. The immigration reform debate of the
past several years has focused on what to do with those immigrants currently living, working, and studying in the United States. In political
cartoons and social media memes, it has been noted that Europeans are
the original undocumented migrants. The cartoons played on stereotypical images of Indians and Pilgrims, where the Indians appear settled and
established, while the Pilgrims are either on a ship or attempting to cross
onto the land. Chicano political cartoonist Lalo Alcaraz has played with
the motif in several cartoons.

Alcaraz depicts Europeans crossing onto land that is inhabited and does
not belong to them. A wooden fence mocks the solution to illegal immigration often touted by politicians, a solution that is not only hostile but
futile, because it won't stop immigration from happening. The pilgrims

ended up in North America just like many undocumented citizens end up in the United States. In another cartoon, a father, wife, and child are holding hands, a reference to the caution signs often visible in towns and cities near the Mexico–US border. To increase drivers' awareness that migrants might be crossing streets and highways, California posts signs that have become iconic symbols in the immigration debate (Fig. 12.1).

Just as illegal immigrants are always being watched by the United States, Native Americans knew about European arrivals to the Americas.

Cartoons such as Alcaraz's and memes in social media make several things clear:

- People with European heritage who want to prevent others from migrating are being hypocritical; their ancestors' arrival in the Americas was not vetted or approved by any indigenous Nation.
- The original (and ongoing) conflict between Natives and European settlers reminds us that contemporary undocumented citizens have indigenous roots.

Fig. 12.1   Caution sign example.

- The fact that undocumented citizens have indigenous roots suggests that most Latinxs, whether considered legal US citizens or not, also have indigenous roots.
- Immigration into the Americas is therefore an indigenous issue.
- Colonization turned immigration upside down, making Native Americans strangers on their own lands and installing Europeans as owners.

Understanding how the United States constructs its borders reminds us that the land is under military occupation. What holds borders firmly in place is their militarization, as well as the continuing legacy of killing indigenous people to prove supremacy and assert sovereignty. It is of a piece with the US practice of breaking treaties and removing indigenous people from their homelands.

White settler occupation sets the terms for who belongs and who is a stranger. White supremacist logic establishes borders and thus justifies the removal and elimination of all non-White bodies unless they align with the system built to control and even destroy them. Anzaldúa's theorization of the border, specifically of what it means to be an atravesado, speaks to the vulnerability all Latinxs face regardless of legal status. In this sense, all Latinxs are considered mojados unless they assimilate into whiteness.

My great-great grandmother, Damitas, was a Tigua Indian who lived along the Rio Grande. My grandmother, Gloria, told me that U.S. officials informed Damitas that she would have to move in order to respect the boundaries drawn by the United States and Mexico. She refused and held her home as long as she could.

For the generations of indigenous people who have lived in the Americas, the borders currently set in place hide the long history and tradition of migration. In response to Arizona's anti-immigrant law, SB 1070, First Nations United—an activist organization organized by Red Lake/Ojibwe and Dakota Indians—released a statement that made the rounds across Native American websites and blogs in 2010. First Nations United denounced SB 1070 on the grounds that the law racially profiles "people of American Indigenous background" and that it is automatically invalid since it is enforced by a settler colonial government (naisa. org). They continue: "As an indigenous organization, we recognize that indigenous peoples from Latin America have every right to migrate up and down the continent as they have done through trade and communication routes since time immemorial" (naisa.org). This press release was shared across Native news outlets, academic websites, and activists' blogs, reso-nating across Native communities.

To be a mojado also is to be marked by forces outside of you. It is the denial that migrations have always existed in the Americas. People move back and forth, and they always have. It also means that those with privilege can move back and forth. In addition, it means that borders are erected to prevent people from coming in and marking as deviants those who do. It also means that those borders make it more likely for people to remain within them and never leave. The borders slow down natural migrations, but they do not stop them. This is a legacy of marginalization and death that is tied to the colonization of the Americas and the estab-lishment of systemic white supremacy. It is thought of as only existing against immigrants, but it extends to the rest of society.

BEING A PERSON OF COLOR AND STRUGGLING TO ATTAIN LEGITIMACY IN ACADEMIA

Latinxs were never meant to be accepted in the US academy. In fact, only white men were ever meant to be accepted. The structures, institutions, and traditions of academia were all designed for white men, and we con-tinue using many of them still. Academia makes adjustments according to changing times and demographics, but this only is done to satisfy public opinion and bottom lines. If we begin with the premise that Latinxs were never meant to be allowed into the ivory tower, then we can see that a border exists to regulate who gets in and who gets to stay in.

If we see the academy as an extension of the colonization of the Americas, originally for white men, then we can begin to understand why students of color feel so marginalized. The majority of students are white. The majority of the professoriate is white. The majority of the curriculum is white. This unfamiliarity makes academia a foreign land. Those who sur-vive are few in number. Those who fail return home in shame, and often with substantial debt.

At the heart of this discussion is how legitimacy is conferred on bodies. This legitimacy is tied to citizenship, which privileges who gets to enjoy the rights afforded by the United States. This is a particularly contentious issue for Latinxs and other people of color in academia. Bonnie TuSmith, an Asian American professor, states that women of color faculty face the largest obstacles toward tenure because of their subjectivities along the lines of gender, ethnicity, and race. The infamous slogan, "last hired, first fired," is known across academic circles.

TuSmith writes about her own experiences in the classroom and describes how students process what she argues is cognitive dissonance in reaction to her presence as the professor. She lays out the following script:

- Professors are white men. You are not a white man. Therefore, you are not a professor.
- English professors are white. You are Asian American. Therefore, you cannot be an English professor.
- Asian Americans are quiet, humble, and submissive. You have strong convictions and you are not humble. Therefore, you are a failed Asian American. (123)

TuSmith adds that this process is racist victim-blaming: she is being blamed for not fulfilling students' racist expectations. The borders are clearly drawn that allow one to be perceived as a legitimate professor in the classroom.

Student evaluations present another problem, as professors of color score lower than white professors. They drop farther when professors talk about any form of oppression, especially racism. Professors of color are thus in a dilemma because their options are limited. They could avoid teaching and discussing *race*, but that would be teaching to the evaluations, compromising many professors' ethics. They could teach sensitive topics and plan frequent activities (e.g., journaling and pressure release sessions) that allow for students to release tension and process their individual conflicts; however, this would be another form of teaching to the evaluations. Morever, any of these could marginalize the original course material, which could lead to bad evaluations anyway. Professors of color could decide to accept bad evaluations and live in peace, knowing that they have kept their ethics and values, but they might hurt their case for tenure.

On the other hand, one of academia's dirtier secrets is that, although departments may discuss the importance of teaching and service, in many places research wins tenure. Yet even here, race and racism intervene. Lewis R. Gordon, an African American professor of philosophy, shared his struggle for tenure at Brown University despite his stellar record. Expectations were already high: "published monograph, several articles, satisfactory teaching, service and signs of international recognition" (truth-out.org).

When he came up for tenure, Gordon's case offered "three monographs (one of which won a book award for outstanding work on human rights in North America), an edited book, a co-edited book, 40 articles (several of which had gone in reprint in international volumes), two teaching awards and service that included heading a committee that recruited 23 scholars of color to the university." His case took longer than usual "because of continued requests for more referees," which increased to 17. A white colleague was also up for tenure in the same department (philosophy) and did similar work to Gordon. His dossier contained a book contract that didn't see a publication until years later, and some articles. Yet this colleague easily won tenure.

Gordon uses these examples to point out how mediocrity plays into white privilege. He asks: "Was investment in white supremacy necessary for less than stellar whites to be promoted? Yes." He points out that while affirmative action critics argue about the fairness of promoting unqualified minority candidates, they never mention the unfairness of mediocre white candidates regularly attaining opportunities and promotion. They also never mention "the group of blacks and brown people who [are] excluded on the basis of their excellence." People of color working in the academy who appear to be "uncontrollable" often find themselves excluded from it no matter how talented and exceptional they may prove to be. White supremacy is alive and well in academia.

MOJADOS IN ACADEMIA

Can people in academia be mojados? With reservation, I would like to return to Murillo's theorization. He is in a difficult position, as am I. People in academia do not take the same risks as undocumented immigrants, at least not nearly to the same degree. So it would be an insult to say that crossing into academia requires the same effort. For Murillo, the term "best describes both the current socio-political and academic distresses, as well as the heroic yet costly successes, of ethnographers, who are chicano/Mexicano, pan-latino, womanists, feminists, working-class and/or other scholars of color" (21). He locates this relationship in the "inequality of mobility and movement across borders" that Chicanx scholars face with issues such as publishing research in reputable outlets, teaching in predominantly white classrooms, and facing unfair tenure and promotion expectations.

Murillo's metaphorization of the term *mojado* is compelling because Chicanxs in academia often cross into unfamiliar places; many of us are the first in our families to go to college or earn advanced degrees (including the Ph.D.). Our legitimacy is constantly questioned by staff, students, faculty, administrators, and campus police. Furthermore, during the last several years, the DREAMer movement has made visible the many undocumented college students who endure the mojado tag on multiple levels. Finally, many are the children of both legal and illegal immigrants, have extended family and friends who are undocumented, and have been called *wetbacks* on campuses.

I remember going to an exhibition soccer game between the women's team of my undergraduate school and the Mexican National Team. Both teams had Mexican and Mexican American players on their squads. A white student was heckling the Mexican team, yelling racial slurs, including "mojados."

On another occasion, a friend of mine was walking to her class, and she heard the students behind her mutter the word "wetback" and giggle, thinking that she couldn't hear them.

As a graduate instructor at one of the most conservative campuses in the country, I established friendships with students who, having seen a chicano college instructor for the first time, confided to me the constant anxiety they felt as undocumented immigrants on campus. During that time, my mother admitted to me that after she and my father married, she spent the first years of her marriage in the United States as "technically illegal," but denied she was a wetback. Although she had a passport to cross back and forth, she did not have resident status. In my first year as a tenure-track assistant professor, I have been Dr. del Hierro, Dr. Hierro, Professor, Marco, and Marcus. I don't know who these people are because I'm Dr. Marcos Del Hierro. In my first two semesters, I have had at least one moment during office hours where a student questions my credentials. One student asked me if I understood the point of his paper as if I were incapable of truly understanding what he meant. Another student wanted an explanation of my policies beyond the clearly written ones available on the course syllabus. Both questions seem innocent until one sees the racist coding that informs them. Add "because you're not white," or "because you're Mexican" at the end of each sentence and see the difference.

Murillo's metaphorization is useful, but I would like to complicate and extend it. According to white supremacy, all people of color are illegitimate. How we are rendered illegitimate depends on the labels imposed on our bodies as a result of skin color, phenotype, accents, and ethnicities. For Chicanxs and other Latinxs, part or all of our illegitimacy renders us foreigners, strangers, trespassers, and atravesados. And ya'll heard what Anzaldúa said they do with atravesados. And because we are all considered mojados, our struggles are tied together. The vulnerabilities, dangers, and difficulties that migrants face, whether crossing national, academic, or other kinds of borders are all informed by white supremacy and colonialism. So we need movements that recognize our mutual desire for the right to live a dignified and good life regardless of ethnicity, nationality, gender, sexuality, ability, or class.

To walk the tightrope of privilege and appropriation, Latinxs in academia need to recognize that, although we have some privileges, real dangers follow us. These include stress, anxiety, lack of sleep, and depression. They also include microaggressions from all kinds of people on campus, as well as mental, physical, emotional, spiritual, sexual violence committed by faculty, staff, students, and police. They include feeling unsafe. They include constantly having their pedagogies; scholarship; service; and other forms of work questioned, interrogated, and delegitimized.

As Gordon noted, any scholars of color who are seen as uncontrollable will be treated as threats. Many professors and graduate students resort to self-medicating through alcohol, drugs, and other risky behaviors. Add to this the fact that we endure a cultural stigma against mental health healthcare, which makes it harder for some of us to seek counseling or medical help. All of this means that surviving academia on every level is a hustle, much like making it across the border. It also means risking much now in the hope of establishing prosperity for the future. And it is happening on land that belonged to "immigrants" all along.

Economists Brian Duncan and Stephen J. Trejo study what they call "ethnic attrition," the declining rate of identification with one's ethnic and national origins relative to how many generations of one's family have lived in the United States (1). Their research suggests that although immigrants to the United States strongly identify with their ethnicity and country of origin, second and third generations experience rising rates of ethnic attrition. For children with Mexican parents, ethnic attrition goes from 5 % in the second generation to 19 % in the third (35–36). Duncan and Trejo also identify a correlation between ethnic attrition and level of education. They write, "...[T]his selectivity arises primarily because Hispanics who marry non-Hispanics tend to have higher education levels than Hispanics who marry endogamously" (36).

The data in this chapter attests to how people are socialized through several institutions, including education, which in turn points to some high stakes emerging over the next decades. The idea that the United States will become a brown nation is now a chorus heard across news outlets; however, even though the nation's population may become browner, this does not mean that white supremacy will end. Opportunistic gatekeepers will continue the process of tokenization and assimilation that reinforces normative whiteness. The poor will continue to stay poor, while the rich will continue to get richer. None of this bodes well for those of us who find transformational potential in education.

WORKS CITED

Anzaldúa, Gloria. *Borderlands/La Frontera: The New Mestiza.* 3rd ed. San Fransisco: Aunt Lute, 2007. Print.

Duncan, Brian, and Stephen J. Trejo. The Complexity of Immigrant Generations: Implications for Assessing the Socioeconomic Integration of Hispanics and Asians. *Centre for Research and Analysis of Migration Discussion Paper Series* 01/12 (2012): n. pag. Web. April 1, 2013.

First Nations United. First Nations United Statement Against SB 1070. *NAISA.* 2010, April 27. Web. July 23, 2012.

Gordon, Lewis R. The Problem with Affirmative Action. *Truth-out.org.* Truthout. 2011, August 15. Web. April 1, 2015.

Murillo, Enrique Jr. Mojado Crossings Along Neoliberal Borderlands. *Educational Foundations* Winter (1999): 7–30. Print.

TuSmith, Bonnie. Out on a Limb: Race and the Evaluation of Frontline Teaching. *Race in the College Classroom,* eds. TuSmith and Maureen T. Reddy, 112–125. New Brunswick, NJ: Rutgers UP, 2002. Print.

INDEX

Note: Page numbers followed by 'n' refers to endnotes.

CPI Antony Rowe
Eastbourne, UK
January 08, 2020